Along the Niger River

AN AFRICAN WAY OF LIFE

TEXT AND PHOTOGRAPHS BY
Aylette Jenness

THOMAS Y. CROWELL COMPANY · NEW YORK

I have drawn on the knowledge and help of many people in making this book, and give my appreciation here:

To Jonathan Jenness, many of whose ideas I express;

To other members of the Kainji Lake Research Project, Food and Agriculture Organization of the United Nations;

To past and present writers on West Africa's savanna peoples;

To friends who read and criticised the manuscript;

To the editorial staff of Thomas Y. Crowell;

To friends and strangers in Nigeria, those who helped me to get where I wanted to go and those whose pictures and stories appear here—my thanks for their help, my pleasure that they are themselves.

Designed by Barbara Hall

Manufactured in the United States of America

1 2 3 4 5 6 7 8 9 10

Library of Congress Cataloging in Publication Data
Jenness, Aylette.
  Along the Niger River: an African way of life.

  1. Ethnology—Niger Valley—Juv. lit.
1. Ethnology—Nigeria. 2. Nigeria—Social life and customs I. Title.
GN653.J46   301.29'66'26   73-20061
ISBN 0-690-00514-8

To those on either side of me—
my parents, Shelby and Richard
my children, Evan and Kirik

Contents

The Past

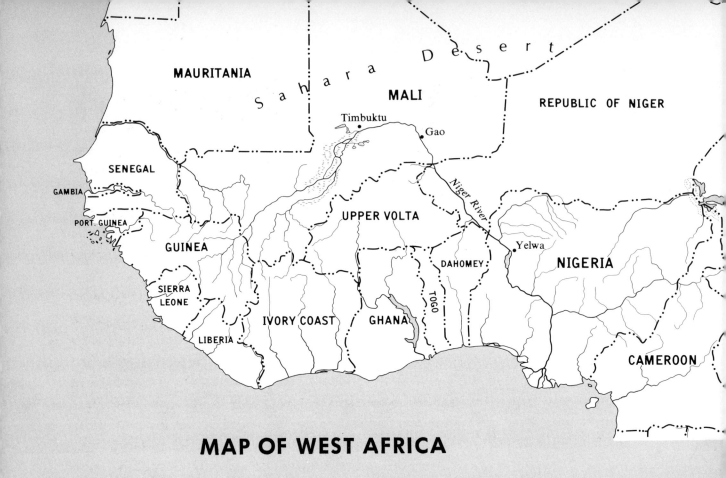

MAURITANIA

Sahara Desert

MALI

REPUBLIC OF NIGER

Timbuktu

Gao

SENEGAL

GAMBIA

PORT. GUINEA

UPPER VOLTA

Niger River

GUINEA

Yelwa

NIGERIA

DAHOMEY

SIERRA
LEONE

TOGO

IVORY COAST

GHANA

LIBERIA

CAMEROON

MAP OF WEST AFRICA

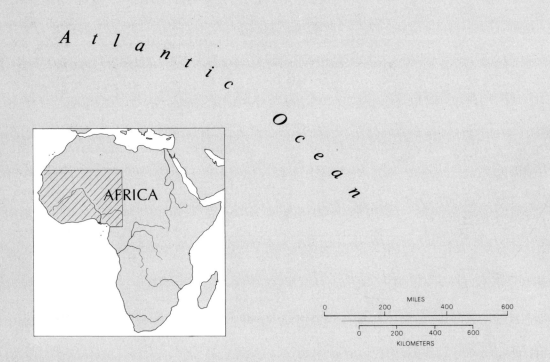

Atlantic Ocean

AFRICA

MILES
0   200   400   600

0   200   400   600
KILOMETERS

The Niger River winds for more than two thousand miles across the breadth of West Africa. It is so long and changes direction so radically that early European explorers, who heard of its existence in widely different places, thought it must be several separate rivers. But it is a single great highway to the people who live along its banks, and has carried their news and goods for thousands of years.

The Niger begins to flow near the Atlantic coast in what is now the country of Guinea. It curves north into land where little rain falls, where the sun bakes the earth almost continuously. Here the trees become fewer, more gnarled, scrubbier. The thick mat of brush gives way to plains of tall grasses—green in the brief rainy season, gold and brown the rest of the year. The river meanders up through this country into Mali, spreading out in swamps though an area of low flat land. Leaving the swamps, it continues north to the edge of the Sahara Desert, where the narrow fringe of vegetation it nourishes along its banks is the only strip of green in the hard sunburnt landscape. Near its northernmost reaches stands an ancient trading center, the city of Timbuktu.

Curving south again, the river flows through the Republic of Niger and down into the savanna country of northern Nigeria. Here it passes through the region that is the subject of this book—the grassy plains, scratched with trails of nomadic cattle herders, the scattered clusters of round, thatch-roofed houses, villages of farmers and fishing people, and the busy trading town of Yelwa. At Yelwa the river slows and widens into the vast new Kainji Lake. Eighty miles farther south, its waters roar through

Kainji Dam, and head south toward the coast once more, toward an area of heavy rainfall and verdant growth. Nearing the Atlantic Ocean, it scatters into a huge delta complex of twisting streams and dense mangrove swamps, a place of hot bright sun on the treetops, hot dark shadow beneath. These streams, silt-laden and sluggish, empty at last into the warm ocean, in the crook of West Africa.

People of many tribes, speaking many languages, following many religions and customs, have lived all across this huge and varied landscape for thousands of years. Some people, particularly those near the coast where movement is difficult, were settled in small groups knowing little of the world beyond their own territories. Others, particularly those in the savanna—the wide belt of grasslands stretching across West Africa between the coastal rain forest and the Sahara Desert—were part of huge black African empires whose rulers raised armies, collected taxes, and controlled trade over territories far larger than many countries in Europe.

The ancient kingdom of Ghana, not to be confused with the modern country of the same name, is the earliest empire of which we have any descriptions written at the time. It was flourishing by A.D. 800, west of the bend of the Niger, and is described with admiration and envy by Arabs from North Africa and Spain, who heard of or saw its wealth and power. The rulers of ancient Ghana controlled a territory of more than 250,000 square miles, and reputedly could send two hundred thousand soldiers into battle for defense or conquest. The royal palace was said to be built of stone and wood, decorated with paintings and sculpture, and fitted with glass windows.

One of the kings is described by an Arab writer of the time in this way:

When he gives audience to his people, to listen to their complaints and set them to rights, he sits in a pavilion around which stand his horses caparisoned in cloth of gold; behind him stand ten pages holding shields and gold-mounted swords; and on his right hand are the sons of the princes of his empire, splendidly clad and with gold plaited into their hair. The governor of the city is seated on the ground in front of the king, and all around him are his vizirs in the same position. The gate of the chamber is guarded by dogs of an excellent breed, who never leave the king's seat, they wear collars of gold and silver. . . .

It is not surprising that foreigners were so impressed with this kingdom, for there was little to compare with it in the Arab world or in Europe at that time. Window glass, for instance, was not used in Europe until several centuries later, and there was no ruler there who could raise an army near the size of that believed to be under the command of the king of Ghana.

This kingdom of the savanna lands, and other later ones ruled by people of various tribes, have been aptly called "market empires," for they grew and prospered on the great trade routes crossing Western Africa. Gold was mined by African tribespeople in carefully hidden places near the coast and was traded by them, along with slaves and ivory, animal skins and cotton, north through the savanna, then across the Sahara, and into the markets of North Africa and Europe. Large numbers of Arab camel caravans bearing European cloth, beads, and steel weapons made the dangerous but profitable Sahara crossing from north to south. Copper and salt from the desert mines were also carried into the south; salt was so valuable that it was said at one time to have been exchanged in equal weight for gold. The rulers of Ghana stood in the middle of this trade, and grew wealthy by taxing the caravans for whom they maintained safe conditions of travel. Contemporary accounts stated that the king of Ghana exacted "the right of one dinar of gold on each donkey-load of salt that enters the country, and two dinars of gold on each load of salt that goes out." The people of the savanna lands—farmers, fishermen, craftsmen—prospered by selling their own manufactured articles and food staples to traveling merchants.

In the eleventh century the empire of Ghana was overrun by Moslem invaders from North Africa, but the trade and tribute patterns were not destroyed. In fact they grew stronger, and later native rulers of the savanna lands became famous throughout Europe for their extraordinary wealth. The greatest of these was Kankan Musa, the powerful black emperor of the kingdom of Mali, which at its height was larger than all Western Europe. His armies extended his boundaries until Mali included not only the taxable caravan routes that crisscrossed the empire of Ghana, but also many of the *sources* of this profitable trade—the salt and copper mines of the north and the gold mines of the south.

Kankan Musa's predecessors had been converted to the Moslem religion by earlier northern invaders. By his reign, beginning in 1307, it was the religion of those in power across the whole of the savanna lands. When Kankan Musa decided to make the long trip eastward across the Sahara to Mecca, a pilgrimage which is the aspiration of every devout Moslem, his entourage was so fantastic that tales of it were still amazing Europeans a hundred years later. It was said that he traveled on horseback, preceded by five hundred slaves, each carrying a staff of gold weighing over four pounds. Sixty thousand followers accompanied him—his wives, soldiers, slaves, and servants, as well as a large group of scholars literate in Arabic. His camel train included nearly a hundred loads of gold, each weighing three hundred pounds. He poured so much gold into Egypt, both by gifts and by buying goods there, that he flooded the market in Cairo, lowering the value of gold for some years. Accounts written at the time in Egypt, and later in Europe, praised his dignity, generosity, and piety. On his return from Mecca, he stopped at Gao and Timbuktu, thriving cities near the bend of the Niger, and had several beautiful mosques for his people's worship built there.

By 1500, Timbuktu had become a well-known center of Arabic learning. There was a university with many scholars in residence. A contemporary historian, Leo Africanus, writes: "In Timbuktu there are numerous judges, doctors and clerics, all receiving good salaries from the king. He pays great respect to men of learning. There is a big demand for books in manuscript, imported from Barbary. More profit is made from the book trade than from any other line of business." Much of the study in Timbuktu was of traditional Moslem religious texts, but records of the time also list scholars who were great travelers, geographers, and writers of original works. Two manuscripts have survived until today; they are detailed accounts in Arabic of the history of the savanna peoples. In the 1500's, Timbuktu was under the political control of Songhai, the last of the great savanna empires. The Songhai emperors ruled most of the length of the Niger River, beyond it westward to the Atlantic coast, and far north into the Sahara.

Then in 1591, Moroccan armies swept down from North Africa, captured Timbuktu and the other large trading centers, pillaged villages and towns, and broke the power of the Songhai Empire. The Moroccans maintained control for only twenty-five years, but the savanna lands were never again such a huge political unit. Several tribes in several places gained dominance over their neighbors, creating a number of rival kingdoms. The volume of trade, which had nourished the earlier empires, shrank as improved European sailing vessels facilitated the shipment of goods by sea around the coast of Africa, instead of in camel caravans across the Sahara. Wealth and commerce in the savanna declined, while Europe during the next two hundred years began a period of rapid technological achievement.

In the nineteenth century, Europe and the United States were hungry for expansion—fresh sources of raw materials, more markets for their manufactured goods, and a cheap labor force of slaves. Helpless against guns and cannon, the savanna and the rest of Africa were soon parceled out. Modern boundary lines cut across ancient tribal and political areas as the European powers dictated.

The country of Nigeria came into being under British rule early in the twentieth century. For the people that this book describes, living in the northern part of the area, the British were not the first outside rulers. These people, of many different tribes, had been organized for hundreds of years into a number of small states under the control of Hausa tribesmen. Somewhat peripheral to the great empires of

Ghana, Mali, and Songhai, many of these states had from time to time owed political allegiance to other, smaller savanna kingdoms. Then in the 1800's, Moslem members of the Fulani tribe took control of almost all the Hausa states, and joined them in an empire under Islamic, or Moslem, leadership. These states still exist today as emirates, territories under the care of emirs, or Moslem leaders. The emirs have lost most of their political power to the federal government of Nigeria, but they are still influential as traditional religious leaders.

In spite of the decline of the great savanna market empires, these states had managed to maintain their ancient trade links with North Africa, Europe, the southern coast of West Africa, and Egypt. Hugh Clapperton, an English explorer struggling into the region in the 1830's, found in a thriving market town silks from Cairo, beads from Venice, and salt from the Sahara. These small states had none of the complicated technological inventions of Europe; yet Heinrich Barth, coming in the 1850's from the factories of industrialized England, saw much of value in their way of life. Speaking of the cloth-weaving trade in a northern Nigerian city, he said, "The great advantage of Kano is, that commerce and manufactures go hand in hand, and that almost every family has its share in them. . . . If we consider that this industry is not carried on here, as in Europe, in immense establishments, degrading man to the meanest condition of life, but that it gives employment and support to families without compelling them to sacrifice their domestic habits, we must presume that Kano ought to be one of the happiest countries in the world. . . ." And this description fits much of Nigeria today.

In 1960, after less than a hundred years of British rule, Nigeria became an independent country with its own black government. In spite of its recent tragic civil war, it is a prospering and energetic country, utilizing patterns that have survived for many hundreds of years.

In Yelwa, a northern Nigerian town of five thousand people, and in the surrounding countryside of Yauri emirate, one sees many of these old patterns, still useful, still working. Today, as centuries ago, many tribes share the area, speaking different languages, pursuing different occupations, and following different religions and customs. Often human beings are suspicious and distrustful of those unlike themselves, but here there is an atmosphere of tolerance and cooperation. Each tribe specializes in a particular form of food production—farming, fishing, herding—or craftwork and trade. Each therefore depends upon the others to supply many wants.

Tribes are united by this need for exchange, and also by their common acceptance since ancient times of an elaborate, far-flung system of government. The small tribesman today is distant from the head of the government of Nigeria just as his ancestors were distant from *their* rulers in the time of the old savanna kingdoms; but the links between peasant and ruler continue to be strong. A man is part of an extended family where several generations live together, and he accepts direction from the senior member of the household. The senior man in turn is responsible for his compound's behavior to the village head. The village head settles disputes, apportions land, supervises common work, and collects taxes for the district head. The district head reports to his superior, and so on. The distant ruler has

Fulani tribespeople lead their cattle past Kainji Dam.

changed over the centuries, but the system has remained intact, and makes possible a large and well-ordered political unit.

Today as in the past new ideas and methods have been absorbed by the people without destroying their fabric of life. Centuries ago, the Moslem system of credit and record keeping was adopted by local peoples, and strengthened their patterns of trade. With the British came Western technology—all sorts of hardware from trains to flashlights—and methods of mass manufacture more efficient than hand production.

The latest change here has been dramatic. In the 1960's a huge dam to generate electricity for much of Nigeria was built across the Niger River south of Yelwa. Kainji Lake, a man-made reservoir of nearly

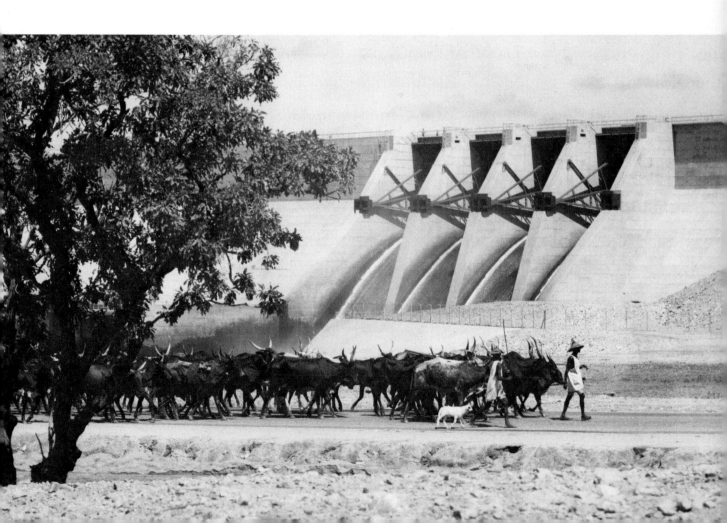

five hundred square miles, spread over the savanna land. Birds found themselves nesting in trees that were largely underwater; wild game fled or was drowned; farms and grazeland were submerged; and fifty thousand people were resettled in new villages.

In Yelwa, at the head of the lake, half the town went under. The palace of the emir of Yauri, the traditional Moslem ruler of the emirate, crumbled and fell into the rising waters. The massive arched entrance halls, with their twenty-foot-thick adobe walls, returned to their original mud. Behind were revealed the meeting rooms, the courtyards, the private quarters of the emir's wives and children, hidden from public view since the year they were built. Government funds provided a new palace of

Palaces of the emir of Yauri: the old and, on the opposite page, the new

gleaming white stucco on higher ground. The emir, an urbane gentleman who was educated in a British university and is active in Nigerian governmental affairs, is as at home there as he was in the palace of his ancestors. His people bridge these worlds, modern and traditional, equally successfully.

In many countries, for many peoples, the introduction of Western technology has been overwhelming, wrecking traditional values and ways of living for the individual and the culture. Examples are endless; the Indians and Eskimos of the Americas are among those we know best. Exceptions are rare, but here in this remote corner of Africa is one. It is not a picturesque anomaly in the twentieth century, but a small profound world with much to show us, if we have eyes to see.

Tribes of
the Countryside

The Farmers

This is not an easy land in which to live. Common parasitical diseases cause blindness, dysentery, and death. Most people are weakened by malarial fevers periodically. Many infants and small children die of malaria.

It is true that two of man's basic requirements for survival are fairly easily met here. Need for clothing is minimal; one could survive with only a covering against the chill of the night. Need for shelter is only slightly more complex—shade from the heat of the sun and protection from the seasonal rains. But food production—farming, herding, fishing, hunting, and gathering—requires much time and effort.

The savanna land at first seems dry, stony, and inhospitable. For nearly half the year, starting in November, no rain falls. The countryside lies flat, open to the full heat of the sun, broken only by occasional low rocky hills and narrow green borders of vegetation along the Niger and its tributaries, and the shores of Kainji Lake. In December the harmattan blows—a parching, dust-laden wind from the Sahara. It brings weeks of cold nights, hazy days, and a layer of desert sand that coats everything, is gritty in the mouth, drying to the skin.

In February and March, as week after week passes with no rain, with midday temperatures of over 100 degrees, the grass withers and dies, and most of the leaves on the trees shrivel and fall. The land becomes so hot that dust devils form—heated spirals of air that twist and swirl across the countryside, pick-

17

ing up lumps of dry earth, stones, leaves and twigs, rattling them around and around, and then scattering them again.

At this season there is no fresh graze available for the nomadic Fulani tribe's cattle; they cannot survive on only the thick, tough, withered grass. So, adding to the heat and haze and dryness, Fulani set fire to unfarmed areas of the countryside, burning off tracts of grass and brush, and charring the trunks of the scraggly fire-resistant trees. Hunters of other tribes fire the bush to drive out small game, and farmers burn to clear new fields. Flames flicker day and night across the landscape, and their crackle mingles with the brittle sound of hot wind in the leaves and twigs. Sahara dust falls on ash; the land is gray, charcoal black, iron red, and tan. The sunlight is diffuse but constant, and the earth is hard as stone. Fulani burn the land because they know that a tiny crop of tender new grass will spring up in a few weeks, and that with the tough mat of old grass gone, their cattle will be able to graze. These bursts of brilliant yellow green look as startling across the countryside as did the fires before them; it is hard to believe that there can be enough moisture stored in the roots of the grass to provide a fresh crop.

This would seem to be a most difficult land in which to raise food, but through the centuries the tribes who farm have developed a system of rainy-season agriculture that is simple in technology, using neither oxen nor donkeys and only a few hand tools, yet utilizes the environment with skill. They produce a wide variety of food by double cropping—planting a field with two successive crops in one growing season—and interplanting—raising several different crops together. Farmers can raise enough food to nourish themselves, and with a fairly varied diet. They also can produce a surplus to feed the nonfarmers of the area—herders, fishermen, traders, and craftsmen—thereby gaining money to buy whatever goods they cannot produce. And finally some of them raise crops for export outside the region, notably the red onions that are prized throughout Nigeria for their flavor.

To grow this amount and variety of food requires time-tested knowledge. In some senses the land here is fragile. Its fertility is quickly exhausted, and farmers have learned to use a field for a few seasons and then allow it to lie fallow, to return to natural growth and regain nutriments. The alternation of a searing, cracking dry season with the torrential downpours of the rainy season means that the thin layer of topsoil is easily washed away, and jagged gullies are cut where the land slopes. Farmers avoid hilly sites and leave a few trees standing in their fields, which help to hold the soil in place. The Nigerian government agricultural service is promoting some useful modern farming methods in a modest program. Fertilizers are offered for sale at subsidized prices so that farmers will be encouraged to try them, to see for themselves the increased yield of their crops. But the funds available are limited, and innovations are accepted slowly.

Luckily there is ample land here for all who wish to farm, and a system of tenure has grown up that ensures a reasonable distribution and protects both the countryside and the people from exploitation. All land within the jurisdiction of a village is considered to belong to that village. A man wishing to farm applies to the village head, who allocates to him as large an area as he can farm, or if the man has a large extended family and perhaps a few young single hired men, as much as they all can farm. To a great extent, need determines use. Ownership as we know it does not exist, for fields not used return automatically to the common village land.

In addition to their crops, farmers raise a few fruit trees that have been introduced from southern Nigeria—oranges, pawpaws, guava, and mangoes. The agricultural extension service is raising these from seed and cuttings, and sells the young trees to farmers at minimal cost. Mangoes have adapted so well that they now also grow wild, and people eagerly collect the fruit hanging in abundance from the large, dense, shiny-leaved trees.

Unlike many farmers in the world, the people here do not depend solely upon cultivated crops; they also forage for a large number of plants growing wild in the bush—for food, medicine, and working materials. They gather the fruit of the tamarind, sop, and date trees. The seeds of the shea tree are laboriously processed to give an oil, or butter, which is used both as food and as fuel for lamps. The leaves of the gigantic baobab tree are eaten in soups and stews, while the bark makes strong rope and the fruit is soaked in water and squeezed to make a refreshing drink. The leaves of the locust bean tree are similarly gathered, and in such quantities that people sell the leaves they do not need in Yelwa market as a cash crop. The material around the seeds in the pods is removed for a food, and the pods themselves are mashed for use as a fish poison. Silk-cotton trees are plentiful, and the large plump pods are collected for their kapok, used in stuffing pillows and mattresses and for caulking canoes. Three species of palm yield food, medicine, wine (for non-Moslems), rope, and

A young farmer prepares his land for planting.

wood. Particular grasses, reeds, and bushes are made into mats, ropes, fish traps, and containers of all sorts, from flexible baskets for carrying grain to large openwork cages for transporting fowl.

Dry and scraggly as the bush looks, it is a rich mine for those who know how to work it.

The beginning of the yearly farming cycle is marked by the activity of local blacksmiths. Near the end of the dry season, the village smithies ring day after day with the beating out of new hoes. The countryside is scoured for strong forked branches, and the hammered metal blades are firmly attached. In late March the men and many of the women go out to prepare their fields, so that planting can begin with the first rains. Slowly, laboriously, the dry soil is loosened. This is a hard enough job if the fields have been cultivated the previous season, and a far more difficult one if fallow fields or entirely new ones must be cleared of brush, deep-rooted savanna grass, and most of their trees.

At last, when the air itself seems to snap and crack with every wind, when the sweat evaporates from people's bodies almost as quickly as it forms, at last the rain clouds begin to gather. Gradually in April the air becomes moist and heavy. Then in May the rains start—some sudden squalls, some thunderous downpours, some slow, soaking, steady. The dust is washed off houses and people, trees and plants, and becomes soft earth once more.

In May and June the farmers begin sowing the main subsistence grains—sorghum and millet. This must be timed carefully—as early as possible to take full advantage of the rainy season, but not so early that seeds will germinate in the first sporadic show-

21

ers and then wither because the rains are not yet steady. Field corn and a kind of quick-ripening millet are next planted in small fertile fields along the river and stream banks. In July farmers sow rice and peanuts, both for home use and for sale. Rice is raised in low-lying moist fields, mainly by women, and is in such demand that it is all sold in local markets, none goes outside the region. The peanuts raised here form a small part of Nigeria's great export of peanuts and peanut oil which are used in many distant parts of the world.

Farming families plant small vegetable gardens close to their homes. They raise okra, peppers, tomatoes, and several green leafy plants for spicy stews to accompany the large amounts of rice or cereal that make up the main meal of the day.

By August it is time to harvest the field corn and early millet, and prepare those same fields for onions, which can be irrigated during the coming dry season. Dry-season farming here is a speciality of one tribe, the Gungawa, but is spreading to others. Small fields by the Niger River, its tributaries, and Lake Kainji are carefully laid out in grids of shallow irrigation channels. Each of the small squares formed by the intersecting channels is enclosed with a low earthen wall, so that the amount of precious water needed for irrigation can be carefully controlled. Then the onion plants, which have been started first in seedbeds, are set in place, one by one, within the squares. This is a great deal of hand labor for a plant that bears only one fruit. In addition, many of these fields are planted along the edges, or later interplanted, with hot peppers, cassava, tobacco, tomatoes, and sugarcane, to take full advantage of the good soil and irrigation.

A Gungawa boy works in his family's onion fields.

In September, the wettest month of the year, as much as ten inches of rain may fall. In November, none at all. Irrigation thus begins in October, when the rainfall drops sharply. All the men and boys of a family work together. The strongest scoop water from the river or lake into calabashes—large hollowed-out gourd bowls—and dump it into the main irrigation trough. Whether done by hand or with a simple wooden lift, this is heavy work that cannot be kept up continuously for more than fifteen minutes at a time. As the water begins to course through the channels, the young boys and old men move around the fields, guiding the water into one square of onions after another. By hand or hoe they make an opening in the walls of each square, allowing the water to flow in, until each has received just the right amount—enough to nourish the onions, but no more than necessary—for the work is hard and long.

Water runs through the irrigation channels as this young boy opens an earthen dam.

Gasoline-powered pumps save many hours of hard work.

The agricultural extension service in Yelwa has been buying gasoline-powered water pumps and renting them to farmers for irrigation. These pumps can be moved by hand along the water's edge, pulling water from river or lake and pouring it through long hoses onto the fields at a rate far faster than a man can lift water by hand. This old farmer, carrying a hoe exactly like the one his grandfather used and tending a new pump, is typical of the contrasts here today, and more important, of the melding of new with old.

In November the busiest time of the year for the farmer begins. The days are bright and hot and cloudless. The grains grow, swell, ripen, bow down their stalks. Millet, peanuts, and the first onions are harvested. They are eagerly bought in Yelwa, and at high prices, too, for the old stores are scanty. In

December the big harvest of the sorghum crop begins. Whole families work together to bring in the heavy sheaves of grain. They fill the adobe granaries in their villages and set up storage platforms in the fields for the overflow. Women thresh the sorghum, beating the sheaves with long sticks to separate grain from stalk, and then pound it in large wooden mortars to loosen the tough outer husk that covers each grain. Women and children separate the kernels from the chaff, or husk, by the age-old method of pouring the grain from bowl to bowl. The wind carries off the lighter chaff, and even the goats share in the abundance, nibbling it as it falls.

In February and March the last onion crop is harvested. Some plants are allowed to go to seed. The seed is then carefully collected, dried, threshed, and stored in glass bottles for next year's planting.

Everyone works on the harvest.

For farmers here, as for most around the world, the time of greatest leisure comes after the time of hardest work, and is perhaps enjoyed the more for that. Harvest is celebrated with the making of great pots of local beer; malted, ground sorghum mixed with water is fermented into a warm gruel, which is flavorful and alcoholic. Moslems are forbidden to drink any alcohol, but most of the farming tribes follow their traditional religions which have no such prohibition.

Many villages hold wrestling tournaments at harvest time. The matches start off with the two smallest boys in the village, watched and refereed by an older man. The winner wrestles the next bigger, and so on through the afternoon, while families and friends gather around, drink beer, go off to do chores, and come back to watch and cheer some more. At last a champion emerges, the most skillful of the

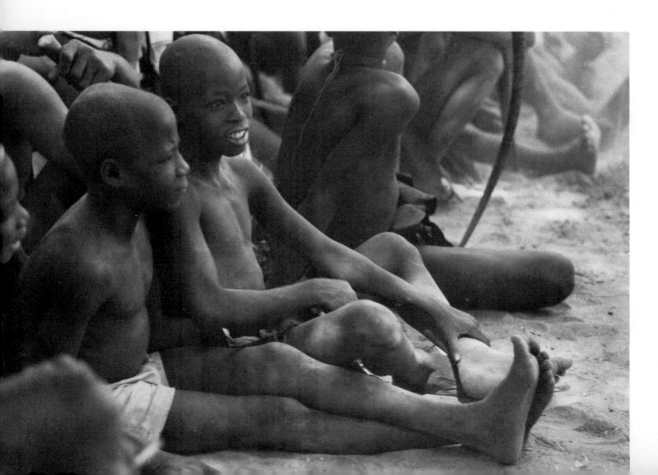

Village wrestling matches

young men. In other communities a kind of traditional boxing tournament is held, and in every settlement people dance to the music of flutes and drums day after day and long into the cooler nights. The line of dancers is always graduated from the most skillful down to the littlest, those skinny-legged boys or girls who miss steps, bump into each other, swing out of line, but are an accepted part of the whole.

The farming people are of several tribes. Gungawa, Lopawa, Dukawa, and others live in villages of several hundred people each, scattered across the countryside and along the river and lake shore. They are slowly, steadily, and uneventfully assimilating the latest outside influences—the world of Islam and of Western technology.

Kamberi, farming tribespeople who live in smaller

A Kamberi hamlet

communities, are somewhat different from the others. Less open to change, more set apart, theirs is a small, cohesive society that seems to be puzzling to others and immensely satisfying to themselves.

Kamberi live in circular hamlets of related families, surrounded by their fields of sorghum and millet. These compounds are a study in cylinders and cones, from the round shape of the adobe houses with their conical grass roofs to the smaller granaries to the little shelters for chickens to the circle of round cooking pots in the open center. A Kamberi hamlet looks as if it is turning inward; a circle is a closed shape. There are no windows or doors on the outside. The spaces between the houses are filled with fencing of sorghum stalks, leaving only a single narrow opening where people can leave or enter. A Kamberi hamlet looks private, insular, a bit defensive, as though expecting attack yet not really strong enough to withstand it.

So with the Kamberi. They were captured and enslaved in the past, so often that they became in effect a sort of crop to more powerful tribes. They were sold south to African slave dealers, resold to white men on the coast, and exported to the West Indies and America. They were sold north, too. As "pagans," they were considered legitimate prey by Moslems and were seized and trekked across the Sahara into North Africa and the Middle East, as dreadful a trip as the Atlantic passage. And as settled farming people, relatively defenseless in an area subject to periodic intertribal wars, they were taken and used as domestic slaves, a long-established custom, in their own land. The ruler of an emirate adjacent to Yauri, famous for his slave-raiding, is believed to have said when warned by the

British to stop, "Can you stop a cat from mousing? When I die, I shall be found with a slave in my mouth." Today, Kamberi are shy, easily startled, a bit humble, yet dignified and tenacious in their adherence to their own culture.

Kamberi are easily distinguished from the other tribes of the region. They are very dark, muscular, and stocky. Their appearance repeats the circular motif of their houses. They wear many bracelets and rings of dull silver color, and decorate their clothing —leather and plain wine-colored cloth—with more silver rings. When they dance, it is in large circles around their drummers. In one of their dances the women carry round woven baskets. They do not gesture with them, or put them together, or do

Kamberi musicians and dancers

34

anything else with them. They just carry them—a circle of women, a circle of baskets. Kamberi even shave their hair in concentric bands, and the skin between is sometimes dyed a deep eggplant color, the color of their cloth.

It is easy for other Nigerians, even easier for Europeans or Americans to say, "Look at the Kamberi. How bizarre! They're almost naked; they wear rings through their noses, bones through their lips; they scar their bodies with big welts." To the Western world they have little of the romantic appeal of such "exotic" picturesque tribes as the Masai or the Watusi. To many Nigerians they are a curiosity, sometimes even an embarrassment. Though they are respected as good farmers and hunters, their

35

customs are regarded as amusing, the women ugly, and their unfamiliarity with the modern world as "bush"—backward or primitive.

What about the Kamberi view of Kamberi? Changing and adapting to an influx of new ideas and cultures has been a regular way of life in this area for hundreds of years. For instance, Islam is the dominant religion of the area, and many tribespeople are abandoning their traditional religions to become Moslem. No hindrances are put in the way of conversion. In fact, pressure to convert has come from strong and disparate sources. In the past, Moslem rulers were forbidden by their religious tenets to buy or sell any avowed Moslems, but no such restrictions

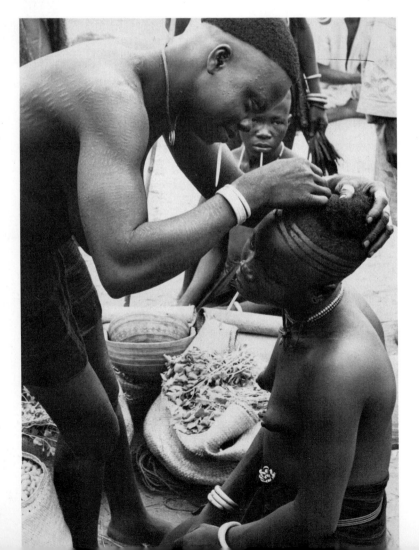

A young Kamberi woman has her hair shaved in decorative circles.

were placed on enslaving "pagans." This was an excellent reason to convert! Also all positions of political power in the Yelwa area are today held by Moslems, and if one has ambitions in that direction, conversion is a necessary step. Yet most Kamberi steadfastly follow their own religious beliefs, as they always have.

Similarly the attractions of Western technology and goods are visible and tempting to many people. Kamberi, men and women both, are extremely hard-working farmers; they are accustomed to selling for cash their surplus crops and the clay cooking pots the women make. Yet what they desire of Western goods is highly selective. A Kamberi man may ride a new three-speed English bike to market, but when he does he will not wear a factory-made shirt. He will put on his earrings, bracelets, necklaces, carry his ceremonial axe over his shoulder, and the tails of his long leather loincloth will wave behind him as he rides. His wife will buy bright green and deep blue plastic bracelets in Yelwa market; then she will cut and file them into crescents to slip through the pierced part of her nose.

The most dramatic influx of Western technology came with the building of Kainji Dam in the 1960's. The British architect in charge of resettlement housing for those who would be flooded out studied the various tribal styles of building. Teams of outside workmen were brought into the region—Nigerians, but southern Nigerians more familiar with the English language, with Western methods of manufacture, with wage-labor jobs and hours. For the Kamberi they built cylinders of concrete blocks covered with a durable material made of cement, sand, and earth—and capped them with domes of asbestos.

These homes would last longer than adobe houses. The roofs would be fireproof and less insect-ridden than grass roofs. Cleaner altogether. Also ethnic; round, like traditional Kamberi houses, and placed in circles to replicate the old hamlets.

Considerable money was spent on housing—the most per family of any resettlement scheme in Africa. Many of the appalling pitfalls of similar programs were avoided—resettling people in housing that destroys their cultural patterns, or in towns too large to be supported by the surrounding countryside, or on land unsuitable to their needs and skills. The Nigerian choice was clearly for the replacement of existing buildings with "better" ones. If a flooded village had a medical clinic, the new one would, too; if not, no clinic. (One village, realizing this, raced to put up a school building before they were flooded out, so that they might have a good new one.)

The money spent on housing could have funded a major upgrading of community services. Many agricultural extension workers could have been hired to expand programs already proving useful throughout the area. More irrigation pumps could have been bought for nominal rental to farmers. More plant nurseries could have been established. Medical aides could have been trained, and clinics built and maintained. Traveling medical teams could have established a program of routine inoculations, like the highly successful smallpox eradication scheme already in effect. Sanitation, health education, infant-care programs could have been started.

But the option was for housing, and housing was duly built.

Some Kamberi liked their new houses, some didn't. Most settled in and began to make the com-

An abandoned Kamberi resettlement village

38

pounds their own. No granaries had been provided, so the people built them with customary skill. Stalk fences were made to fill in the areas between houses.

In one resettlement village, a large extended family was surprised to find that when they were taken to their new compound, they were given half of a circle of houses. They didn't know the people assigned to the other half. This was puzzling. They felt as strange as an American family would if they had bought a house and moved in to find half the rooms occupied by another family. While wanting to maintain good relations, they still tried to restructure their traditional family set-up. A long meandering grass fence was built across the middle to give the two families some privacy. But this didn't really work. A few months later the new hamlet was abandoned.

The family moved to a new location. In the dry season they built their own houses. Mud balls, mixed with straw, grew into walls, were smoothed over, dried in the sun, hardened, became strong enough to withstand perhaps ten years of winds and rains. There was, of course, no need to hire outside builders. Kamberi have been building their own houses ever since there were Kamberi. The tall bush grass was cut and gathered at the peak of its season, and tied into thick rainproof roofs, bound into a tuft at the top. Large stones were set on the ground, and up on these were built granaries, safe from insects and other pests, and from damp in the rainy season.

Inside the compound a cooking place was chosen, and the round clay pots wedged together—the innermost circles of all. Calabashes for bowls and dippers, woven baskets for containers, grass mats for sleeping and sitting—from earth and plants, the hamlet was built and furnished. The family brought

Inside a Kamberi compound

themselves and their few extra clothes—finery for wearing to market and celebrations.

Now settled, the women again make the clay cooking pots they sell at Yelwa market. The old blind father continues to braid the straw rope in which to transport them; it is the only job he can still do. He listens to the sound of his world—grain being pounded, chickens scratching and clucking, children playing, a little music when the daily work is finished, sounds as integral and meaningful to his life as the circles and circles which enclose and keep him, the same sounds and circles that are repeated in each small Kamberi hamlet throughout the area, in patterns stretching far into the past and perhaps well into the future.

The Herders

The farming tribes here are mainly planters and cultivators. They keep only a small amount of live-stock—cattle, sheep, and goats—barely enough for their own use, not enough to supply meat and milk to Yelwa, not enough for export outside the region.

Cattle raising and the sale of dairy products are carried on almost entirely by another tribe—the Fulani. Since foods rich in protein are scarce and expensive in Nigeria, government researchers are trying to see how Fulani cattle raising can be made more efficient, more productive. But the Fulani do not view themselves as meat producers at all—dairy people, yes, for they sell milk and butter, but sellers of cattle only under duress. Although in fact they supply most of the beef eaten in the Yelwa area, and many of their cattle are exported to southern Nigeria, their own goal is actually the opposite of this. Their aim is to have ever-increasing herds, and they are willing to allow their cattle to grow in number until large areas become badly overgrazed. They would like to be able to sell no cattle except the old, the barren, the sick, and to pass on to their children and grandchildren large healthy herds. Only in this way can they hope to continue their own culture and way of life, which they consider superior to all others. Many Fulani also farm, usually with part of the family planting a crop of quick-ripening grain during the rainy season, but they are not proud of this. Everyone pities the Fulani whose herd is so small that the sale of milk cannot bring in enough money to buy grain and who must turn to full-time farming. This precludes his herding, for unlike ranches and dairy farms in many other parts of the world, the land here will not support settled cattle raising—far from it. The cattle must be moved every few days to find enough grass and water to live, and to avoid contracting the many diseases of the area.

The lives of the nomadic Fulani scratch long lines in space and time across the savanna. Originally from the western part of the great grasslands, they have gradually spread until today they live throughout the whole area in many of the modern West African countries. They move in small family groups, each with its herd numbering from twenty to sometimes several hundred cattle, as well as a few sheep and goats. In the dry season, when streams cease flowing, Fulani move into the lush swamps and floodplains of the rivers and Kainji Lake, and eventually southward where the land is greener. Here they must beware of the tsetse fly, which carries a disease that can kill entire herds. The dry season is the most difficult time of year; cattle and people grow thin together. Cows give little milk, people have less to eat, practically nothing to sell, and must trek farther to keep their herds alive. A dry-season greeting between Fulani is, "How is the patience of your family?"

When the rains begin in May, pale spiky shoots of grass emerge from the hard-baked earth and the stream beds fill again. Fulani begin to move toward upland graze, away from the river swamps, and north, away from the tsetse fly area. This is the good time of the year. Cattle eat their fill in smaller areas, in shorter hours. They grow sleek, and firm flesh covers their bony frames. Fulani families can camp near friends and relatives; it is a time of visiting and celebrations, of relief from worry. Even the soaking rains, from which people have little protection, do not discourage them.

Still they must keep traveling. Cattle make places muddy, and then run the risk of contracting foot rot. Vast numbers of flies accumulate. Every few days, during the rainy season, families pack up and move. Their "houses" are easily dismantled shelters of sticks and mats, and their possessions no more than can be packed on a single ox. Men may sometimes have to carry calves born along the way, women, the frail new wobbly-legged kids of their goats. Babies are carried on their mothers' backs; toddlers ride cattle. Everyone else walks, day on day, season on season, year on year, generation on generation, marking the landscape indelibly with cattle trails far older than any roads in this northern Nigerian countryside.

Just as the cattle trails cross but do not follow the network of roads used by other Nigerians, so Fulani live among others and yet are apart. They are dependent upon others for much of their food, and nearly all their material goods—they make practically nothing themselves. Knives, axes, cooking and water pots, calabashes and dippers, clothes, grain, vegetables, even their jewelry and makeup, must be bought. For cash to buy these things, they must nearly every day sell soured milk and butter in village and town markets. Despite this dependency, Fulani are aloof and superior, with a mixture of shyness and arrogance that is disconcerting to non-Fulani. Others say they are like the wind in the bush, passing through, leaving nothing behind but a few bent branches and a bare spot of ground. Fulani say

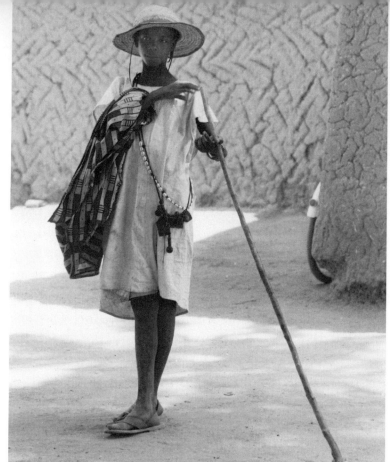

Young Fulani men

of themselves that they are like a flock of birds; touch one, and all fly away.

As their pattern of living differs radically from that of the settled farmers, so does their appearance. One cannot imagine people more different from the solid, rounded, dark Kamberi. Fulani are as linear and angular as their long-horned cattle, as their way of life. Tall, thin, bony, they carry not a spare ounce of fat. The men are seldom seen without a long cattle stick, which they often carry across their shoulders, arms outstretched, long hands dangling. At rest they are apt to stand on one leg, leaning on the stick—a pattern of lines and angles, the stick nearly an extension of the body. Their clothes, which are made for them by Hausa tailors, are white, brilliant green,

and peacock blue, embroidered with pointed ara-
besques in black, red, and yellow. The women move
quickly, dartingly, like birds, and their long pointed
braids swing about, glinting with thin gold orna-
ments. Their delicate linear tattoos on face and
breast are enhanced with cosmetic lines of black and
white dots. Men and women both take a pride in their
appearance which is more than personal vanity.
Pale skin, a straight nose, narrow lips, and a long
neck are characteristics of ideal Fulani appearance
which are as valued as adherence to Fulani values,
and in fact are so bound up with them that a person
may be thought to *be* an exemplary Fulani if his
looks meet these ideals. A Fulani proverb runs, "See
the nose, understand the character."

One group of Fulani has a myth that describes the
essence of their life with great clarity. The origin
tales of many tribes tell of a spirit or god who made
those particular people, where there were no other
humans before them, no humans in the world at all.
For many cultural groups in the world, their name
for themselves means simply Man or the People.
Fulani, on the contrary, who have always lived
interdependently with other tribes, do not see themselves as the first or only people on earth.

The myth begins with a non-Fulani couple who
lived in a small village. The woman had a quarrel
with her husband and in a burst of anger picked up
her young son and marched off into the bush. When
her anger cooled, she returned to the village and to
her husband, but realized that in her confusion she
had left the child behind. She immediately returned
to the bush and looked everywhere, but could not
find him and at last gave up the search.

The boy survived and grew up alone. When he was

46

*A young Fulani girl,
dressed in her finest:
cowry shells and metal
bands decorate her hair.*

47

a youth, a water spirit appeared to him, saying that since he had grown up in the bush, he would continue to live in the bush, but that he would be wealthy. The spirit told the youth to go to the river and wait there until he saw a pure white cow emerge from the water. He must then immediately turn his back and walk away from the river.

The youth did as the spirit had told him. He went to the river; the white cow appeared; the youth turned his back, and walked away for a long time. At last he turned around, and saw that all the time he had been walking, cattle had been coming up out of the water and following him, and that now there were a great many of them. When he turned to look, the cattle ceased to come up out of the river. The last four to emerge were red ones, and this explains why today there are many more white cattle than red.

The youth continued to live in the bush, and he took care of the herd. He married an Arab girl, and their children, the first Fulani, married each other. Their cattle increased greatly in number, and their descendents increased, continuing to marry among themselves, continuing to keep to the bush.

Fulani have been leading their herds ever since, and they liken their lives to that image. As cattle must be protected from wild animals, so Fulani must be protected from the world of non-Fulani. Their ethic is summed up in *laawol pulaaku*, an oral tradition, meaning the Fulani way (literally, "footpath"). Its components are modesty and reserve as ideals of personal conduct, patience and fortitude in enduring hardship, and care and forethought to be a good herder. One must adhere to these beliefs to travel well and safely along the path, and it is indeed a difficult way.

A stranger may pass in the daytime within a few yards of a Fulani camp and never know it is there, so inconspicuous are their belongings, so much a part of the landscape. If he does find the camp, he may think it haphazard, casual. A few sketchy grass shelters, a rope strung between two trees, a trampled circle where the cattle are kept at night. But, in fact, most Fulani camps are set in an exact manner, and this arrangement, like their origin myth, is illustrative of their way of life. Patterns vary from clan to clan, but a particular group will always follow its own particular pattern. The following is a pattern found among Fulani north and west of Yelwa.

The smallest unit that can live independently is a single family, but for survival it must be a complete family—a man, his wife or wives, and their children. They will choose as a camp site a circle of land encompassing if possible some shade trees, some open ground, near graze and water, not more than half a day's walk—fifteen miles—from a village market. Among many Fulani the calf rope, to which calves are tied at night so that they will not drink all their mothers' milk, bisects this area. It separates the men's side of the camp from the women's, and is the only place where they work together, tying and untying the calves. In some Fulani clans, a woman crosses the calf rope only to milk the cows, a man crosses it only to sleep in his wife's shelter. To the east of the rope are the cooking hearths and small bed shelters belonging to the wife or wives of the family and their young children. Behind this is a curving brush fence. This is considered the back of the camp, and women will always enter their camp, or any other, on this side. Men never will.

To the west of the calf rope is the unfenced cattle

corral. At its center is a smudge fire which is kept burning from dusk, when the cattle are brought back from grazing, until dawn, when they leave the camp again. The fire drives away mosquitoes and flies, which are annoying and disease-carrying, and it also keeps wild animals at a distance. Fulani believe the fire has magical properties of protection as well. It is a solemn duty never to let it go out at night, lest ill luck befall one's herd. Around the cattle and forming the westward arc of the circle are the sleeping shelters of the boys and young men of the family, who enclose and guard the herd even while they sleep.

The family is an essential unit for the cattle herding and dairying life of the Fulani, but companionship between man and wife, or between other male and female members of the family, is not essential, and is minimized by Fulani custom. Babies are born into this arrangement, and within it they grow up, though the camp itself shifts often and over a large area of land. Little boys and girls play freely in the eastern side of the camp, and by the age of seven or eight are expected to watch the calves, sheep, and goats which graze nearby. When a boy is about ten, his father takes him into the cattle corral and points out the animals that were given the child at birth, and those which are now to be set aside as his, so that when the boy marries he will have the nucleus of his own herd.

Now the child leaves the women's side of the camp. His father gives him a wooden staff, and a set of charms so that his cattle will prosper. His mother gives him a water gourd to carry. He sleeps by the cattle each night. He herds the cattle during the day, and he spends the evenings talking with the men of the family near the smudge fire. He learns the name and characteristics of each bull, cow, and calf in the herd. He learns the calls of his particular family, and how to talk to the cattle, directing them with clicks, whispers, hisses, and soft words. He learns how to care for them, keeping them free of ticks, putting herb poultices on sores and wounds, splinting broken bones, assisting in birth. He learns about cattle illness, and to avoid diseased herds or areas where sicknesses are apt to be contracted. The men of the family talk endlessly about cattle, and the boy learns their practical lore and their protective magic.

As the boy approaches manhood, he will want some free time to go with his friends to the village markets, to meet girls of families living nearby, and to attend dances of young people. This part of his life culminates in the *sharro*, a ceremonial occasion when young men allow themselves to be beaten by their age-mates to show their stoicism and fortitude. The girls flock to this affair, wild with excitement, dressed in their best clothes, and all their jewelry—a mass of necklaces, glass beads, fine chains, coins, agates. Clustered together, chattering, they watch with admiration. Each of the young men takes his turn at being beaten, standing ready with a posed nonchalance, hand on hip, sometimes holding a small mirror up so that he too can admire his courage as the heavy stocks raise welts on his back. It is illustrative of Fulani values that this test of manhood is one of endurance, rather than of aggressive action.

Now it is time for the young man to marry, usually a girl to whom he has been betrothed since childhood. There will be an exchange of gifts, and eventually the girl will come to live with him in his family's

camp. She will spend her days with the women in the eastern part of the camp, helping with food preparation and chores, but she will sleep with her young husband on the cattle side of the corral in his rough bed shelter.

It is not until she has become pregnant, has gone back to her own family for the birth of her first baby, and returned when the child is weaned at one or two years of age, that she and the young man may, if they wish, set up their own small complete camp some distance away from that of the young man's father. At this time the girl's family gives her the domestic and dairying materials she needs: the bedsticks, polished smooth and stained with red dye; the ropes and mats to complete the shelter; and the pots, bowls, calabashes, and dippers for feeding her family and preparing the milk and butter that it is now her job to sell in the markets. The young man's family supplies their cattle needs—a pack ox that will carry their domestic goods when they are traveling and their own calf rope to which are tied at night any calves that have been born to the cattle earlier set aside for the young man, any calves the wife's family may have given her, and any calves that may have been given to the new baby.

When the first child is old enough to help with herding, the family may, if they want, move completely away from the older generation. This begins the prime time in a Fulani man's life. With care and skill and luck, his family increases and his herd increases. Each is dependent upon the other. The herd must produce enough milk for sustenance and sale; the family must have enough members to care properly for the herd. If the herd greatly increases, the man will be able to marry a second wife, and in

Fulani women

53

fact her work will be needed for dairying. Many Fulani sayings illustrate this symbiosis: "If one harms the cattle, one harms Fulani." "If the cattle die, Fulani die." A large and healthy herd can be acquired only through years of hard work and constant vigilance; but it can be decimated by a single epidemic. Fulani still tell of the rinderpest plague that wiped out a vast number of cattle across the savanna lands of West Africa nearly a hundred years ago. It is said that men went mad, left their families, and wandered unclothed in the bush, eating dust and calling their dead cattle.

As the man's sons grow up and marry and move out of his camp, he may give away more and more of his cattle. He has always thought of his herd in long-range terms; he sees them as a trust to pass on to his children, not as wealth to be used in his lifetime. As the woman's children grow up, marry, and move out, she has fewer mouths to feed, fewer cows to milk, fewer dairy products to prepare and sell. She gives her daughters, as they set up their own households, her pots and bowls, calabashes and dippers; she has less need of them.

Thus the man and his wife or wives end up in old age with few duties, few possessions, and will eventually move into the camp of one of their sons, usually the eldest. If the man has more than one wife, the old people will become separated, for each wife goes to the camp of her own eldest son. Among some Fulani, the old man will have his sleeping shelter to the west by the cattle corral of his son, and he will spend most of his time there. He will die there and be buried there, and the camp will move on. The old women will have their bed shelters in the eastern half of their sons' camps, and spend their time in

those domestic areas, helping with household chores and the care of the little children. When they die, their shelters will be left intact and never used again. They will be buried beyond the brush fences in the eastern part of the camps.

The people and the herds will move on, as they always do, in the order in which the camp is set up. The head of the household will start out, the cattle following and flanked by the young men of the family, then the calves and small livestock flanked by children, then the women leading their pack oxen, loaded with bedsticks, mats, household utensils, and little children—all of them heading, as always, for fresh graze and good water.

The Fishing People

Another itinerant group follows different ways across the savanna. While Fulani provide beef for local use and for export, Sarkawa and Kyedyawa provide fish. The men prefer to be full-time fishermen, and like the Fulani, farm only incidentally or when they must. Their paths are the Niger River and its tributaries, and like the Fulani they have gradually migrated from their original area.

The Sarkawa count as home an area on the Niger a hundred miles north of Yelwa. The Kyedyawa came from a region several hundred miles to the south, and still consider a town there as their headquarters, and the town chief as *their* chief, though most of them have never lived there. For many generations, for several hundred years, they have been moving along the Niger and other rivers, spreading their nets further and further into the territories of other tribes.

In times of intertribal warfare they moved slowly or pulled back to home grounds. After the British conquest in the early part of the twentieth century they increased their territory, until between them they were fishing the Niger upriver beyond Timbuktu, and down to the delta at the Atlantic Ocean, a distance of fifteen hundred flowing, twisting, swamp-lined, island-studded river miles. Seeking new fishing grounds, they first entered new areas by living on their boats, whole families together, for several months at a time. They ate their fish, sold some of the surplus catch to local farmers or exchanged it for grains and other foods, and smoked the rest for resale outside the immediate region. Once accepted in a territory, they began to come in greater numbers, to stay longer, to set up seasonal fishing camps, and, at last, to build permanent settlements, either in spots of their own choosing or as adjuncts to existing towns and villages. During all this time, and even today, they have followed a social pattern strong among Nigerians. They have spoken their own language, followed their own customs—which clearly set them apart from others—and seldom married outside their tribe.

Though they moved into areas belonging to others and maintained their separateness for generations, there is little evidence of friction or suspicion or envy between immigrants and indigenous peoples. Many Sarkawa and Kyedyawa today do practice some farming, and many farming tribes also fish for subsistence and small-scale sale, but this has not produced much competition and conflict. Why?

Sarkawa and Kyedyawa make no claim to the land. They have never considered themselves landowners, sometimes not even of their original territories. Instead they have a strong image of being "owners of the river." They, and other tribespeople as well, believe they have magic that will improve fishing, protect them from disaster on the water, and ward off crocodiles and other dangerous creatures. Their gear allows them to fish in the middle of the rivers, and out on Kainji Lake. Local farming tribes fish primarily the upland creeks, the marginal swamps bordering the rivers, and perennial pools. Sarkawa and Kyedyawa have always respected these traditional grounds and avoided using them, so competition has been minimal. And since fish is always in greater demand than supply, locally and all over Nigeria, its sale causes no financial loss to others.

Perhaps most important, Sarkawa and Kyedyawa have been Moslem for a long time, and thus tied into the political structure of the area. They are attuned to patterns of hierarchy. They know the customs of elaborate greetings, of respect for superiors, of proper behavior.

A group of professional fishermen who moved into the region more recently and less successfully provides an example of how tolerance and cooperation failed. During the last forty years, Ibo and other tribesmen from southern Nigeria, who were ambitious and skillful fishermen, moved north up to and far beyond Yelwa along the Niger. They, however, were Christian in a non-Christian area, and they were totally unfamiliar with the particular customs and formal courtesies of the region. In fact, they regarded northern Nigerians as rather backward, less conversant with the modern world than they who were accustomed to mission schools and Western business practices from their earlier contact with the British near the coast. On the other hand, Sarkawa, Kyedyawa, and other tribespeople living along this stretch of the Niger had for hundreds of years been distrustful of southerners and leery of traveling south into their territory. Ancient cultural suspicions thus were exacerbated by different responses to varying degrees of influence from the Western world. When the Nigerian civil war began in 1967, these Ibos fled or were killed and only very slowly ventured up the Niger again after the war ended.

While the Fulani nomadic cycle is determined by

the rainy and dry seasons, the fishing people's pattern conforms to the regular yearly floods of the Niger, and more recently to the fluctuations in water level of Kainji Lake. The rainy season throughout West Africa falls in roughly the same months, from May to October, though it is longer and heavier near the Atlantic coast and shorter and scantier near the Sahara Desert. But the Niger River is so long that rain falling during the rainy season on the large watershed area of its headwaters in Sierra Leone and Guinea takes several months to flow past the Yelwa area, causing a regular flood. Rain falling in a catchment basin just north of Yelwa produces a flood much more quickly. In addition, the water level of small tributaries flowing into the Niger near Yelwa varies with local rainfall. The height of the lake is determined by man. The flow through the dam is regulated according to the amount of water needed to produce electricity. Thus there is a complicated pattern of rising and falling water levels. Channels, swamps, and pools are flooded, drained, isolated, or dried up at different times of the year, and fish movements and concentrations vary accordingly.

To the uninitiated, this great flow of warm water through hundreds of miles of streams, swamps, and rivers might seem to contain a huge fish population, but this is not so. Before the creation of the lake, an industrious fisherman would not expect to average throughout the year more than a hundred pounds of fish a month. Since the formation of the lake, the number of fish has increased considerably, but the fishermen still move from one area to another seeking good grounds and fishing long hours for a very mixed catch. More than seventy species are sought

A Sarkawa woman near her fish-smoking oven

by day and night, on rising and falling water, all through the year.

The settlements of Sarkawa and Kyedyawa fit into the landscape as neatly as their life patterns fit into the social and economic web of the area. A clear place by the waterside is chosen on ground high enough for good drainage in the rainy season. Men and boys cut poles from the nearby bush and lash them together for house frames. Grass mats, woven by the women, form the walls, and a species of long fine grass makes good roof thatch. Between the houses are fish-smoking ovens made from the clayey earth that is readily found in the area. These are hourglass-shaped, with a fire built in the lower part and the fish laid in racks across the upper. The fully smoked fish are stored under cones of thatch for protection from rain and animals.

There is a mosque in every settlement. Not a building, but simply a swept-bare rectangle of sandy soil oriented east and west. Here people come during the five daily prayer times, often casually; men pray more regularly than women; children, if they feel inclined. When several fishermen have returned to the camp at the same time, they may pray together, but just as often a single man kneels, fingers his beads, prays quietly for a few minutes, and then goes about his work. The "mosque" is delineated simply by a low looping wall of fishnet—and this seems symbolic of the way their religion is an ordinary part of their life.

Fish move silently; fishing is a quiet activity; and boats are powered here only by paddle or occasionally by sail. The tone of Sarkawa and Kyedyawa people is quiet, too, as though an extension of this, and their camps are peaceful places. Men repair their gear, with children watching, helping, or getting in the way. Women talk quietly or sing a bit as they pound grain, cook food, prepare the fish for smoking, or attend to their children. There seems a richness of time and leisure. Often the loudest sound, the greatest motion, is the lapping of waves against shore, the paddling and waddling of ducks and ducklings moving up from the water to forage for scraps of food around the sandy camp.

The fishermen over the centuries have developed a wide variety of gear, most of it made from local materials, well fitted to all the different fishing conditions they encounter.

The great eagerness with which fish are sought is perhaps most clearly seen in a technique practiced by farming tribes—Kamberi, Gungawa, and others. During periods when the water level drops, riverside

Fishermen repair worn gill nets. A woman dresses her child's hair.

or stream-bed pools are left containing concentrations of fish. Farm families often partition these shallow pools with mud walls, and empty them completely, section by section, calabash full after calabash full, until men, women, and children can scoop up the stranded fish. Farmers who live near water also raise several plants and gather wild ones for poisoning fish during this period. People cast these mashed plant fibers into isolated pools and stir the water with sticks. Within a few minutes virtually all the fish there, young and old, rise to the surface of the water, gasping and flopping helplessly about. They can easily be gathered then, and the fish is not

poisonous for people to eat. Obviously this is a poor conservation practice, since it kills off all the fish, leaving none to reproduce. Therefore, poisoning is allowed by custom and by local authorities only in isolated pools that traditionally belong to particular families or groups of families.

Sarkawa and Kyedyawa do not poison, but they and the farmers who fish make a variety of traps with mesh large enough for baby fish to swim through. Each man makes his own traps from local wood, bound with grass and vines. He works at home as he has time, and stores the finished traps safely up in trees until he is ready to use them. Each trap has been devised for particular conditions. Fishermen set the *dago* and *undurutu* in shallow swampy areas where fish swimming around and feeding on the abundant growth will enter the traps accidentally and be unable to find their way out again. The *suru* is placed across a stream between stick fencing; it catches all fish, over a certain size, that move by with the current. The five-foot-long *gura* is tied in deeper water and swings freely; fish swimming upstream enter and are trapped.

Men work together to build huge fish weirs in shallow parts of the river during periods of low water. These are rectangular, one-hundred-foot-long enclosures made of tight stick fencing, which is secured to the river bottom and extends above the surface of the water. They are left open at one end and baited with containers of sorghum chaff. Fish moving upstream enter the open end, and cannot figure out how to reverse direction and escape. Each day the men drive the trapped fish down to the end of the weir and scoop them out of the water with dip nets.

Fish traps hang from tree branches until they can be set in the water.

Throwing a cast net requires perhaps the most skill and endurance. The fisherman goes out by canoe with a boy or young man from his household as paddler to a shallow area where fish are known to be abundant at the time. He gathers up the big net, holding it carefully in his hands. With the retrieving cord tight between his teeth, he twists his body and flings the net into a perfect circle far out over the water. Weighted with lead around its twenty-five-yard circumference, it sinks to the bottom, evenly, quietly, trapping the fish within its area. The fisherman slowly draws up the retrieving cord, and the net becomes a narrower and narrower cone until the fish are completely entangled in the meshes. This work is tiring, and a man can keep it up for only a few hours. Then he is paddled to shore, with the bottom of the shallow dugout full of silver fish—several kinds, big and little; none are considered too small to eat.

66

A lift net catches fish from underneath, the opposite direction from a cast net. The fisherman lowers the net into the water, waits a few minutes, then raises it to scoop up fish moving into the swamps from the main riverbed during the time of rising water.

Sarkawa and Kyedyawa all own longlines, too, baited and unbaited, which they set in many places —along river banks, along and across streams, and in the lake. Some are four or five hundred feet long with several hundred hooks dangling from them. The fisherman checks his longlines every day, sometimes twice a day, sometimes with a boat but often without. He wades along, lifting his line, looking for the silver shape, the movement in the water ahead of him. He grasps each fish firmly, unhooks it, and drops it into the large round calabash that floats beside him. When the water becomes too deep for

wading, he begins to swim along the line, using the calabash as a float as well as a container; the water is never cold, and his clothes will dry quickly on land.

Fishermen also use gill nets, drift nets, and seines with mesh of various sizes depending upon the kind of fish wanted. Drift nets, with floats on the top edge and weights on the bottom, are floated downstream by fishermen in boats. Fish moving upstream swim headfirst into the nets and are caught by their gills when they attempt to back out. Set gill nets work the same way, except that fishermen secure these in productive places and return later to remove the catch. Seines are used to surround fish; men working together lower the nets into the water in large circles or arcs, and then pull them slowly in to shore. Some of these nets are more than three hundred feet long and six feet deep. They are made of expensive and durable nylon webbing with plastic floats and lead sinkers attached, so that they can be set to fish the bottom surface or the top. As lake fishing has ex-

A fisherman prepares his gill net for setting.

panded, these are used increasingly—an adoption of modern technology fitted into traditional patterns by the people themselves.

Fish caught for home use are cooked and eaten the same day. Some are sold fresh in village markets, but in this hot climate, fish begin to spoil after a few hours. There is no refrigeration here, no freezing or canning facilities, so the fish to be sold outside the region, a considerable commercial volume, are smoked, just as they have been for hundreds of years "at home" in Sarkawa and Kyedyawa settlements. The women gut the fish, roll them into coils secured by sticks, and smoke them for several days in their ovens. Fish that are to travel far must be smoked longer; if they have become infested with insects while awaiting transport, they must be resmoked. The men then pack the fish tightly in *mankaras*— one-hundred-pound bundles bound heavily with rope—and bring them by canoe to Yelwa market for shipment outside the region.

Floating on a calabash, the fisherman checks his net for fish.

People
of the Town

A line of steep rocky hills parallels the Niger River where it widens into Kainji Lake. Between hills and water is a close-packed band of tan adobe buildings—the town of Yelwa. Several hundred family compounds form varied patterns. Some are clusters of round earthen houses, each roofed with a heavy conical thatch. Others are rectangular, flat-roofed with adobe, like North African houses. Still others, of the same style, are government-built houses for families whose original compounds were covered by the waters of the lake.

Though houses differ in style, they reflect similar patterns for living. A high blank wall or thick grass-matting fence entirely surrounds each *gida*, or family compound. Built into the single entrance is a small visitors' room, the *zaure*. Here street vendors or acquaintances of a family will stop and call their business; here the head of the family—*mai gida*—will sit and chat with his men friends. Beyond the *zaure*, only women and children go unannounced, for these are almost all Moslem families. The young married women are in seclusion and are not to be seen by men other than their relatives.

The main road running through Yelwa is a narrow belt of green. It was planted by some long-gone British administrator with a double row of neem trees, introduced to the country from India because they are fast growing, and unlike most local vegetation, keep their leaves during the dry season. The trees are big now and meet each other over the wide road, giving a shade so heavy and cooling that it feels like a shower bath compared to the parched heat of the countryside.

On the outskirts of town, on opposite ends of this road, are the two Christian missions. In this strongly Moslem area, the Christian influence has been tightly circumscribed. Mission schools are forbidden, and proselytism is allowed only among the non-Moslem tribes. The Protestant mission is on the southern edge of Yelwa, sitting in an oasis of quiet under the hot sun. The grass grows tall, the buildings are half closed, their roofs sagging. The mission is run in a desultory fashion by a Dakakari tribesman, convert of an American woman missionary who comes to Yelwa now only for occasional visits.

On the other side of town is the Roman Catholic mission, which runs a hospital when a doctor can be found to live there. Wire-fenced, it encompasses a large area of dry stubbly cut grass, raked paths, scattered shade trees. Its low stone buildings are one room deep, windowed on both sides to catch all cross breezes, and shaded by long verandas and carefully watered vines of flowering bougainvillaea. Several hard-working nuns live there, treating the diseases of the area as best they can in their meagerly supplied clinic, whether a doctor is there or not. The emir shows his support by sending the pregnant women of his household to their prenatal clinic—a distinct break with the traditional custom of seclusion. When a doctor is in residence, he finds his job frustrating. Medical help is badly needed in the area, but often patients are brought to him only as a last resort, when in fact they are beyond all help. The death of a patient is a poor advertisement; building up trust is slow work.

Several priests live in another building and travel out into the non-Moslem villages to seek converts, but their effect is nearly negligible as they know.

People are apt to abandon their traditional religions only for Islam.

The center of town, in all senses, is the market, a great open space with stalls running down to the waterfront. Here a deep-water shipping area has been built for barge traffic on the lake. Beside the shipping area is the boatyard, where transport canoes are repaired. Behind the market is the new palace of the emir and a cluster of local government buildings—police, post office, medical dispensary.

Near the hills, on high ground, is the big water storage tank. Some years ago the emir installed a public water supply system in Yelwa, with pipes leading to taps scattered throughout the town, thus ending the necessity for each family to carry water from the river. The primary school is nearby, a one-story barrackslike building which provides elementary education for children whose families want to send them.

Yelwa wakes to the singsong shouted recitations of the boys of the other school in town, where Islam is studied. The chant rises and falls unevenly in the cool gray dawn, some voices piercing and thin, others rumbling hoarse and low. These two dozen boys, whose parents give up their labor at home for the honor of having a son who will be considered a scholar, live with the teacher, or *mallam*, work for his household, and beg most of their food around the town. It is a religious duty and a source of satisfaction to give food or money to the needy or the holy, and here the categories are combined, for the boys are dependent upon the charity of their neighbors. The best student, waving his switch for emphasis, leads the recitation of passages from the Koran, the

In Yelwa, young Moslem scholars read and recite passages from the Koran.

Moslem holy book, exhorting the circle of boys around him to shout more loudly, more vigorously, to show their piety, their seriousness, their knowledge, their devotion to their *mallam*.

The volume rises, the sound reaches nearby compounds, penetrates the darkened closed sleeping rooms of the neighbors. The people of Yelwa begin to wake and rise—slowly, deliberately. No alarm clocks shrill night into day, shattering dreams, tensing people to enter the world.

By the time the din from the Moslem school has died down, the regular, hollow sound of grain being pounded to flour in wooden mortars has begun to come from inside first one compound, then another. Each pattern of thumping, whether distant, light, and shallow, or close and deeply resonant, forms an even unhurried rhythm. Together they make up a morning music, as familiar, as inevitable, as the growing light and the rising sun behind the hills.

Every sound in Yelwa has its time in the day, its place, its meaning, and identifies an activity in the life of the town. The chopping, rasping noise of adze against wood and the higher carrying ring of hammer against metal leads one to the boatyard. Under shade trees, on ground gently sloping down to the waterside, half a dozen men work at repairing the transport canoes that come to Yelwa.

Trees are neither large enough nor numerous enough here to be used for making any but the very small fishing canoes called *kwalle kwalle*. *Abara*, the most common boats in the area, are the dugouts pictured. Each is made of a single log—some are as short as eighteen feet and poled by a single fisherman; some as long as seventy feet, powered by one or two forty-horsepower engines and capable of carrying eighteen thousand pounds of cargo. *Abara* are

Badly rotted canoes await repair in Yelwa boatyard.

80

made far down the Niger near the coast, where the tropical rain forest produces a profusion of big trees.

These boats are very valuable in Yelwa, where so much transportation is by water. Trucks bring goods from southern Nigeria to Yelwa for shipment by canoe to towns as far up the Niger as Timbuktu. Kerosene and manufactured goods from factories in Nigeria, England, Europe, and the United States are carried in this way, along with kola nuts, palm oil, and soap produced in the coastal area. The Yelwa region itself sends clay pots and dried onion leaves upriver by boat, and onions and dried fish downriver.

Skillful hands fit a patch into a canoe.

When these transport canoes become old and develop cracks and rotten places, they are carefully repaired. Some have been rebuilt so extensively that they now seem to be more patches than original hull. The men of the boatyard laboriously cut out all the bad wood, and then shape pieces of local wood or wide milled planks imported from the south. They patch from the inside, using long nails, and caulk the seams with easily obtainable kapok. Three tools are used—imported factory-made hammers and saws and locally smithed adzes. Work is slow.

A need for more and better boats has come with the creation of the lake and subsequent increase in fish. Men fishing where Kainji Lake is wide need boats that will not capsize in a sudden wind squall. Farmers traveling on the lake need more large transport boats to take their produce to villages along the

shores. The boatyard is changing to meet these needs. More sophisticated tools will be used, and plank or plywood boats will be built here. Some men from Yelwa studied plank-boat construction techniques downlake, with a United Nations boatbuilder sent to Nigeria for this purpose. If the boatyard workers follow Yelwa's pattern, they will adapt to new methods without losing their own tempo. The boatyard will be bigger, busier, noisier, but the men will still stop work to eat when they feel like it, to chat with a friend, or to go off and do an errand.

Dundunge is the Hausa name for the small pounder used in shaping Yelwa's clay water storage jars, and it is this sound, soft, monotonous—*dun-dun-gay, dun-dun-gay*—that comes all day long from the rush-walled sheds where the pots are made. Every family in town has one or more of these containers, resting in a shaded corner of the courtyard, holding the water for household needs—drinking, cooking, washing. The same jars are used in distant farming villages, and hundreds are carried by transport canoe far up and down the Niger. Yet all are made by a small group of Hausa tribesmen who work in Yelwa only during the dry season.

Newly repaired canoes along the lake shore

The men come from a town far to the north of Yelwa and return home to farm during the rainy season. They are all relatives for whom pottery making has been a family craft for generations. Of the dozen workers in the group, the oldest is Audu Rashidi, perhaps fifty, and the youngest is his four-year-old son, Umaru.

Audu is nearly blind now. One or another of his sons leads him from their family compound to the worksheds every day, where he spends most of his

83

Yelwa's youngest potters making water jugs

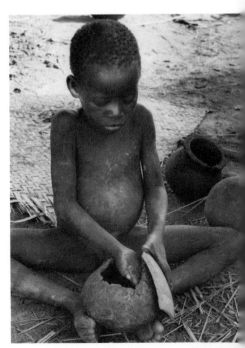

time sitting in the shade of the neem trees. Yet his hands are still skillful, and he helps Mallam and Umaru, his littlest sons, shape their pots. Five-year-old Mallam learned his work by living with it from infancy. His eyes and mind take it in all the time. With a curved bit of calabash, he beats his pancake of clay over an inverted jug made by his next oldest brother; his pot is literally shaped by his brother's. Umaru watches, and with some skill, copies Mallam, using one of Mallam's small jugs as a mold. His production is limited not by his skill but by his interest. He tires quickly, dresses up in a man's hat, naps in the shade.

But Mallam works steadily every day at the pottery, without anyone telling him to or urging him or prodding him. He is a serious child, a little fragile,

84

yet he stops work when he feels like playing with Umaru. The pots he makes are not just for fun or practice—far from it. They are small rough replicas of the big water storage jars his elders make, and they serve a specific purpose. At many praying places in Yelwa, inside compounds and in the small mosques, stand one or more of Mallam's pots. They are kept full of water, and used in the Moslem ritual of washing hands, feet, nostrils, ears, and mouth before prayer. Some people use aluminum teakettles or other containers, but many have pottery jugs, and all these are made by Mallam. This is his own economic niche, filled as well by him as his elders fill theirs. The money from the sale of his pots goes to his family, and is a real contribution now that his father can earn so little.

Pot making begins by kneading chaff, and some water if necessary, into freshly dug, unsieved clay. This husk is a waste product from winnowing grain, and the potters collect it free, along with old sorghum stalks for kiln fuel, from nearby farmers. The chaff helps to hold the clay together while the pot is being formed, and in firing allows the escape of air bubbles, which might otherwise cause it to burst. In addition, the chaff makes a more porous container, which allows for greater water evaporation and therefore cooling when the jar is in use. After Adamu, Audu Rashidi's cousin, kneads this large amount of clay, he forms it into fat pancakes, each one the amount of clay needed for a pot.

These men make their pots by the "paddle and anvil" method. With one hand, the potter turns the pancake of clay quickly around in a shallow concave mold dusted with ash, while his other hand pounds it continuously with the small heavy pestle, *dundunge*. The sides curve quickly up, and when the jar is a hemisphere, it is set aside to harden a little, and another begun. Each potter is surrounded by his circle of containers, waiting for the next step. Here Mamman has brought his pot up almost into a complete sphere, and is smoothing it off. He next puts on the rim, turning the jar deftly in his hand. By this method, each potter can make a large number of pots in a day.

Every man marks his work with his own roulette—simply a nail wound with string, which is rolled around the pot. The difference in the way the string is wound produces a different design, and each man can tell his own pieces, for though they are fired and sold together, each man collects the money for those he makes. The jars are then banded with slip—a creamy mixture of water and clay which is a slightly different color from the clay of the pots. Finally part of this band is polished with a string of smooth hard seeds. This makes a simple decoration, but it is done each time with care and precision.

Mamman's pot is complete.

The kiln is simply a round earthen wall with a few small openings at the bottom. The sun-dried pots, unfired, are so strong that the man loading the kiln from the center can walk out over them when he is finished. The firing, lasting less than an hour, further hardens the pots and causes a chemical change whereby the clay will not dissolve in water. Grass laid on top burns with a fierce heat, and the potters, sweat running off their bodies, take turns feeding sorghum stalks into the bottom of the kiln through its small openings. Next day the kiln is cool. It is unloaded, and the pots are lashed onto crossed sticks and head-carried to Yelwa market.

The materials for the pottery are all free, and easy to come by. There is only one cash expense in the whole business—a small tax when the pots are sold in the market. There is no waste product here, nothing to dispose of except the finished jars: a pair of skillful hands, three or four small homemade tools, clay, grain chaff, ash, sorghum stalks, fire— nothing more. In two days a lump of clay dug near the worksheds becomes an essential item of every household. The method these potters use produces a perfectly spherical pot. This shape, simple and har- monious, is of maximum economy, as a sphere encloses the greatest volume with the least surface area; and this seems indicative of the whole organic, unwasteful nature of this work. The jars are round- bottomed. They sit securely in shallow mossy depres- sions in the earth of the courtyards. When they are

Everyone uses the Hausa potters' water jugs.

taken out to be filled with water, they are carried on people's heads; opposing curves of head and jar are joined by a rolled doughnut of cloth. The jars are unglazed, so moisture evaporates constantly through the sides, keeping water cool on the most blistering hot days. Western technology cannot supply an object to better fill this need.

From roadside stands to the market, from the boatyard to the pottery, Yelwa's streets and open spaces are full of activity. Behind the compound walls is another world, equally varied, equally productive, but hidden from public view. Yelwa's Moslem married women, though in seclusion, nearly all have businesses or trades, and the money they make is their own, not turned over to their husbands. A considerable volume of the manufacture and commerce in Yelwa is conducted within and between compounds, with men, old women, and children serving as intermediaries or retailers.

91

This compound has three generations of cloth-makers, or at least two and a watcher-learner. It's an old compound, surrounded with grass fencing, full of heavy shade trees, dotted with three or four small round earthen houses for storage and sleeping. In this climate many activities are outdoor. There is a thatch-roofed cooking place where a fire smolders continuously, and near it the water jars stand. Off to one side, behind a fence, is the pit latrine. A few chickens scratch the hard-packed soil, and a goat being fattened for a Moslem celebration is tethered under a tree. It's nearly always quiet here, for the family is small. Tasks begin early, in the cool time, in a leisurely way. When the sun is hot overhead, the women put aside their work and sleep awhile.

The grandmother spins thread from locally raised cotton by a method used around the world for thou-

Grandmother, mother, and daughter all work at cloth making.

sands of years. First she attaches a bit of cotton from a ball of the cleaned plant fibers to a stick weighted with a small bead of clay. Then, holding the loose cotton in one hand, she spins the stick with the other. This twists the fibers into a thread, which is then wound onto the stick by another twirl of her fingers.

The completed thread is taken to a dyer nearby, and then the old woman's daughter uses it to weave cloth for wrappers and robes. Though Yelwa market is full of machine-made yard goods, and even tailored clothes, people will still pay a substantially higher price for a good piece of handwoven material in a familiar and favorite pattern. The granddaughter learns the trade in that oldest of all schools—a childhood of watching her mother and grandmother, of doing bit by bit those parts of the work for which she is ready.

The compound where the weavers live is one of the smallest in Yelwa. Mallam Baba's is one of the largest. There are nearly thirty members of the household—from Mallam Baba to Tani, his youngest daughter. The household represents penny capitalism at its most intricate. Not only does every adult member follow a different moneymaking trade, but many members buy and sell raw materials among themselves, and some hire others to manufacture or sell the finished product. In its closely interwoven social and economic relationships, the family is a microcosm of all Yelwa.

94

Mallam Baba is *sarkin kifi*, chief of the fishermen of the emirate. In this role he gives advice, settles disputes over fishing rights, and dispenses the magic necessary to use when hunting crocodiles. At home he is *mai gida*, head of the household. Like many Moslems, he has more than one wife. His two wives are called by almost everyone *Mai Tuwo* and *Mai Fura* after the cereals that they prepare from pounded grain. In their late forties, they are now considered as old women who need not be in seclusion. Mai Tuwo goes to market to buy her grain, but has enough customers nearby to work at a stall in front of her house. More gregarious, Mai Fura sells around town and in the market herself.

The seven children of Mai Fura range from a daughter of thirty, who lives with her trader husband in Ghana, to little Tani. In between are five sons, all at home. Of Mai Tuwo's six children, three are married daughters who live, as is the custom, with their husbands' families, and three are sons at home.

Several of Mallam Baba's younger brothers live in his compound. Warra is an agent, a middleman between canoe owners and those who wish to find transport for themselves or their goods upriver to the countries of Niger and Mali. Tondi, the next brother, owns his own large transport canoe. He buys Kamberi pots, and when he has a load of several hundred, takes them upriver to sell. Most of his time is spent on his boat with his family, but he considers Mallam Baba's compound his home. There are other male relatives in residence; one owns a smaller canoe and runs it as a ferry, bringing people to Yelwa market and returning them to the other side of the lake in the evening. Another has a food stall across the road from Mallam Baba's house and sells sugarcane, cigarettes, and kola nuts to those coming into Yelwa. Still another is a contractor; he hires workers to dig sand and gravel outside Yelwa and bring it to town for sale to local builders using cement.

The wives of each of these men have their own work. One is young and in seclusion. Her husband buys peanuts for her in the market and has them ground there by machine. She then presses the oil from the "peanut butter" and bottles it, selling to neighbors who send a small child to fetch it. The leftover pressed mash is also sold, to a neighbor who makes *kulli kulli*—hard, chewy fried pretzels. Another wife buys fresh fish each day from Mallam Baba's son, Nuhu. She cleans and fries it, and since she has no children herself, she hires Sale, a ten-year-old boy of the household, to hawk it about the streets for her. Who is Sale? He is Mallam Baba's daughter's husband's other wife's child. He lives at Mallam Baba's simply because he likes it; there are always a lot of things going on here!

Mallam Baba moves through his bustling world with dignity, surety, and humor. Short and powerful, he stands with his legs well apart, and the soles of his feet are nearly as hard as the ground on which they rest so solidly. His movements are deliberate and unhurried, whether he is doling out beancakes to a circle of clamoring children, or moving his beads at prayer, or resting quietly in his courtyard. He manages the diverse affairs of this large household with quiet skill, from supervision of the three or four fishermen who are given room and board in exchange for a large part of their daily catch, to such matters as arranging the marriages of his children.

Most delicate of these last has been the wedding of

*Mallam Baba's son,
Nuhu, and Nuhu's wife
at work in the compound*

his son, Gado, one of Mai Fura's children. Nuhu, Mai Tuwo's eldest son, gave Mallam Baba no trouble. He is a quiet, gentle, and responsible young man of twenty-five. He is a conscientious fisherman, turning over most of his catch to the household, selling the surplus to his aunt. He married the girl whom Mallam Baba had picked out for him, and she has proven to be a good wife—hard-working, skillful, amenable to direction from the older women of the household. But Gado—Gado has always been a bit wild and undependable. He spends his days with a crowd of unmarried young men in the town, and his nights who knows where. He is never to be found when needed, and at twenty-two he contributes very little to the household financially. Mallam Baba hopes that marriage will settle Gado down. Typically, Gado wants to choose his own wife. Bahi, sixteen years old, is a girl of suitable family, and very pretty. Unfortunately her parents made arrangements years ago for her to marry another young man, and as she approached marriageable age, the usual presents were given to her parents by the young man's family. When pressed by Gado to negotiate for Bahi's hand, Mallam Baba refuses to be hurried. He slowly sets about learning the feelings of all concerned. He finds out that Bahi, in love with Gado, has refused to marry her fiancé. This sort of tough-minded independence does not indicate that Bahi would make the most dutiful of daughters-in-law, but Gado is interested in no one else. Mallam Baba learns that Bahi's parents are distressed that they cannot control Bahi, and embarrassed because they have accepted gifts from the young man's parents. Mallam Baba learns that, under the circumstances, the young man's family does not want Bahi as a daughter-in-law, but that they expect recompense for their gifts. He then begins, very delicately, to visit Bahi's compound.

Many an evening he puts on one of his best robes, and walks the length of Yelwa to sit in the *zaure*, the visitors' room, exchanging the long customary greetings, talking quietly or sitting in silence with Bahi's father. Then he is invited into the courtyard, offered a cigarette or coffee. He greets Bahi's mother, watches Bahi as she goes about her tasks—bringing water, tending the fire, washing dishes. When it is clear that a match can be made, Mallam Baba starts to marshal his resources. Now begins a series of visits to other compounds. With tact, he lets it be

Mallam Baba's married daughters, home for their brother's wedding

98

known that he needs a return of the money he has loaned an old friend starting a business. A relative gives Mallam Baba a large sum to help out; Mallam Baba helped him in a similar situation some years ago. Mallam Baba puts gentle pressure on the members of his own household to contribute. Slowly the store of coins and bills hidden in Mallam Baba's room grows. He purchases cloths, livestock, and other goods for gifts to the family of Bahi's old fiancé as recompense for their original outlay.

At last a day is set for the wedding, and Mallam Baba has a scribe write a letter to his married daughters in Kontagora, a distant town, telling them to come home for the celebration.

In a few weeks the girls arrive, the elder, aged twenty, bringing her little daughter with her. They have gifts for their parents and wear all their best clothes to show that they are well provided for in their husbands' homes.

Tall, languorous, lean, these two girls are a striking contrast to the other women and girls of Mallam Baba's household. They move so slowly that the pattern of their motions can be easily followed with the eye, and so gracefully that a chore, like sweeping the compound, assumes the beauty of a dance. In their elegance of movement and gesture, they remind one of high fashion models; but as soon as this comparison comes to mind, one discards it. Seen in this light, fashion models seem paper imitations of that real elegance which is born of surety of self.

The women of Mallam Baba's family pound grain on Gado's wedding day.

The first music of Bahi and Gado's wedding day is the early morning grain pounding in the courtyard, the sound growing, echoing in neighboring compounds. On this occasion all the women at Mallam Baba's pound together, not because it is more efficient but because it is more fun. Four or five at a time spell each other, setting up rich and subtle rhythms varying with the weight of the pestle, the hardness of the grain, the inclination of the pounder, the heat of the sun. When they tire of that, two women pound together, each throwing up her pestle between beats and clapping her hands, or, as a variation, striking the pestle against the side of the mortar, the intricate patterns of thuds and clicks slowing down and speeding up as they tire or are

101

urged on by watchers. One of the girls turns an empty calabash over in a larger calabash of water, and drums lightly and delicately on that. When enough grain is pounded they rest, gossip, go off to their rooms to wash and dress and ornament themselves.

An occasion like this wedding shows at its fullest the Moslem girls' lifelong orientation toward making themselves attractive to men. Baby girls are tattoed or marked on the face with the parents' tribal scars, their ears are pierced for tiny gold earrings, and they are apt to wear a bright beaded belt, anklets, or bracelets. Little girls dress like older girls, in as brilliant a variety of patterned clothes as their families can afford. Little girls watch older girls putting on makeup for an occasion and do the same—kohl under the eyes, a long black line emphasizing eyebrows, even lipstick. These young girls enjoy a great deal of freedom before they marry and then, abruptly, are in seclusion; the opposite of our traditional Western pattern of keeping a young girl from the world, particularly from possible love affairs, before marriage. An unmarried Moslem woman is an anomaly; there is no place for her in the society. The career is marriage—the only other one open to her is, tellingly, prostitution. Girls marry young, at fourteen or fifteen. Upon marriage a girl moves into her husband's family; if she wants to end the marriage, she must leave any children she has borne with him. Where can she go? She can marry another man, and this often happens. She can return to her own family, but they are apt to welcome her only for a temporary stay. So marriage is the path, and girls prepare early for it, by learning household skills, and by making themselves as attractive as possible.

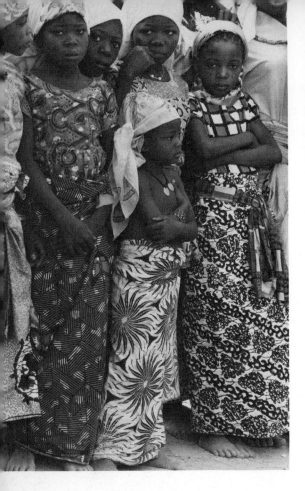

On the day of Gado's wedding, drummers come,
and girls of the neighborhood, dressed in their finest.
They dance some dances given only by girls coming
into marriageable age, which are openly seductive.
The dancers avert their heads in a formal affectation
of shyness, and move torso, legs, feet, quickly, pro-
vocatively, in time to rapid, insistent drumming.
Little girls watch seriously, learning. Boys and men
enjoy. Older women pay little attention; they are
through with all this.

Later the older women of the household do some
dances particular to fishermen's families, in honor of
Mallam Baba's status as chief of the fishermen.
Gado's mother, Mai Fura, is urged out into the
center of the gathering, and dances with such skill

and dignity, though she is heavy now and dances rarely, that everyone smiles and cheers her on.

At last evening falls, and Bahi is brought in a flurry to Mallam Baba's, where she kneels in Gado's room, with her scarf drawn shyly over her head, while friends and her new relatives troop in and out to welcome her.

Her bridewealth, or dowry, comes with her, and in a few days it is put in its permanent place, lining the walls of her and Gado's room. The dozens of enameled bowls and trays, plates and saucers, the covered brass basins, transform the bare tan walls into a vibrant mosaic of flowers and animals, of geometric patterns and mottoes. By day a shaft of sunlight from the door lights the rich reds and blues, bright

Mallam Baba's new daughter-in-law with her bridewealth.

yellows and greens; by night the flame of a single lamp softly illuminates the small glowing jewel box. These were accumulated for Bahi slowly during the years of her growing up, and some are from her own mother's bridewealth. The older ones, decorated with pale delicate birds and branches, were imported into Nigeria from China, making the long journey by freighter, train, and truck. Newer ones, very vigorous and bold, are made in Nigerian factories; huge imaginary tropical flowers and bright stencilled words celebrate Nigerian Independence (1960), exhort the literate to support the country, and remind one that "No Condition Is Permanent." Bahi will use a few of these containers for cooking, but most are a permanent decoration, never touched, showing her status as the daughter of a prosperous family.

Mallam Baba's hopes seem to be proving right. Married now, Gado is settling down. He stays home at night and works more regularly. Mallam Baba is

Mallam Baba and his prospective wife

turning his attention to a new matter. He is beginning a new series of evening visits, a new gathering-in of resources. He has decided to take another wife himself, a young one, the daughter of an old friend. She is shy, but most amenable to the idea.

Mallam Baba's youngest daughter, Tani, is the smallest thread in the rich pattern of this household, and within it she has her own place, her own activities, her own slowly expanding world view.

As an infant, she spent much of the time tied snugly against the small of her mother's back. She moved with Mai Fura's body as chores were done—pounding grain, tending the fire, cooking food. The motions were varying, but seldom sudden, nor were transitions sudden. Asleep or awake, there were nearly always the same people, the same sounds and sights about her—her mother, her father, her father's senior wife, Mai Tuwo, her half sisters and brothers, her own brothers, her aunts and uncles. She seldom left the compound because her mother was then in seclusion.

As the youngest of the thirteen children of the household, she was looked after, played with, enjoyed, passed around. There was nearly always someone free to attend to her needs, though this was often done casually, quickly, sometimes brusquely, but not with anger or dislike.

Now six years old, she is beginning that great age of freedom that northern Nigerian Moslem girls enjoy until they are married. Tani can make her way all around town, knows the turnoffs along the half mile of main road to the slaughterhouse, the dye pits, the water station, the agricultural offices and nurseries. She knows Yelwa and its happenings in a personal internal way. She does not question adults much, nor tell them much. They are not very interested in her words. Her access to adult knowledge is largely limited to what she deduces from her own observation. She is not given the simplified explanations of complicated matters that are passed on to Western children through schools, books, television, and conversation with parents. She is tough. If hurt, she does not get a shower of attention, does not expect it. She is small, wiry, linear, fairly strong. She does not have the swollen belly that comes from an enlarged spleen due to malaria, though she has fevers from time to time. She has no soft fat on her, feels all angles and bones, though she is graceful in motion and in repose.

She has the particular sophistication, independence, skill in getting what she wants, that in America is found usually among poor children—urban street kids—which is not surprising, for she shares their freedoms, though not their neglect or poverty or brutalization. Illiterate, nonverbal, unanalytical, she radiates confidence, awareness, sensitivity, surety, curiosity, humor, delight. When crossed, she shows some sadness, more annoyance, modified by a cool knowledge of how to escape censure, how to get what she wants. She is self-contained, above all.

Tani is enrolled in Yelwa's elementary school. Sometimes she attends; she isn't pushed very hard about that yet. Her real school is the town. Her education is not a preparation for life; life is her education.

She has a business, of course. Mai Fura mixes some of her own dough balls with sugar and water to make a warm gruel. Tani hawks this about town, carrying on a head tray the big bowl of *kunu*, a

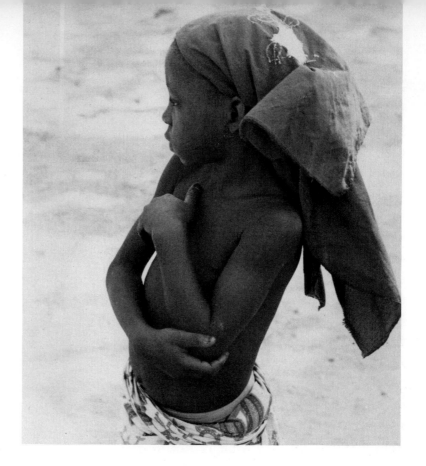

Tani surveys her world.

dipper, and the small bowls for customers. She makes accurate change from the little store of coins knotted into a cloth under her wrapper.

She often sells to the Hausa workers at the pottery, where she stops to finger a bit of clay, to play with Umaru and Mallam, to watch the men. Her favorite and most profitable place of sale is the market, where her world expands to its widest horizon. She has never gone outside of town, and in a sense she doesn't need to do so: so many people come to Yelwa. The market is the great meeting ground, the place of exchange of goods and gossip, the place where she sees the onion-raising Gungawa tribespeople, the dark Kamberi, the shy angular Fulani, the fishing Sarkawa and Kyedyawa, and the merchants of Yelwa itself—a place of infinite interest to all.

Yelwa Market

In countries where people still exchange their goods in markets, every town and village has its own day when the market meets there regularly. These days are carefully staggered, so that itinerant sellers can travel from market to market with their goods and the people of nearby towns can attend each others' markets. Each market is the center of an invisible circle encompassing an area of farms and hamlets of which it is the trade center.

A village market combines the features of American shopping centers, restaurants, of factories, warehouses, and transportation depots. It also serves the functions of our newspapers, radio, and television, for news and entertainment. In a market one can buy anything and everything from a box of matches to a bicycle. One can have a shoe mended, have one's hair done, and visit with a friend who lives in another town. People feel strongly about their markets, for if they are full and busy, the people will be able to sell their goods easily and buy whatever they need. In Nigeria markets are spoken of as though they were living creatures. If the building of a new road bypasses a town, leaving it without easy access, the inhabitants say mournfully, "Our market is dying." If another town's market increases in popularity, and one's own loses business, the people will say indignantly, "Our market was stolen!" Many markets are believed to have a spirit who protects them. The spirit may inhabit a large tree in the market, and people trading there will leave small offerings so that the market will flourish.

Yelwa's market has been steadily flourishing for many decades, for it is the center of a trading web

113

whose strands reach far up and down the Niger River, far along the main road through the area, far out into the countryside in all directions.

Early in the morning of market day, while the air is still cool, merchants and craftsmen within the town begin to bring their wares to the marketplace. At the Hausa pottery sheds the men and boys tie their water jars onto crossed stocks and carry them carefully down the main road.

Even earlier, at dawn, the country people rise, pack their goods for sale, and start the trek to town. Kamberi hamlets for a radius of ten or more miles around Yelwa are left in the care of children and old people as their men and women set out with baskets of grain and stacks of clay cooking pots. Gungawa and farmers of other tribes load into canoes the red onions grown in irrigated riverside plots, along with other farm crops in season—tomatoes and greens, hot peppers, rice, and millet. Some gather bundles of fresh grass to sell as fodder for goats and sheep kept in Yelwa compounds. Sarkawa and Kyedyawa men pack smoked fish into their boats and start to paddle to Yelwa. In small cattle camps scattered through the bush country, Fulani women prepare their soured milk, while the men decide which among them will go to the market to gather news from other Fulani about conditions of water and graze in nearby parts of the area. Fulani young people put on their finest clothes and start the long walk to see friends with the same sense of excitement that American teen-agers feel when heading for a party or the neighborhood hang-out. Along road, river, and path, by foot, truck, and boat, hundreds of people slowly begin to converge on Yelwa market.

The market center is a large open space of hard-

114

*Unloading produce
by the lake shore*

trodden earth dotted sparsely with shade trees. Dozens of stalls are set up here each market day. Some are merely cloths spread on the ground and heaped with one family's produce; others, more substantial, are grass-mat covered structures of poles. The most substantial are the rows of concrete stalls built by the Nigerian federal government to replace those flooded by the lake. Ringing the market are the slaughterhouse, the truck depot, the stockpiles of dried fish, the wholesalers' onion sheds, the boatyard, and the lake shore.

The lake shore early becomes crowded with canoes of all sizes. Huge ones from Mali and the Niger Republic, which serve as homes for the families of

their owners, are filling up with goods to be sold far upriver. Small canoes ferry farm people and their produce across the lake. Here Kamberi women unload their clay pots and baskets of grain. Among all the tribal women in the area, only they carry on their shoulders; they load each other with burdens so heavy that one person cannot lift them alone, and head for the market, stooping under the weight.

Bundles of smoked fish ready for transport by truck.

Gungawa onion farmers carry some of their produce directly to stalls in the marketplace, and the rest to large open sheds by the waterfront. Here, under the shade of grass matting, the heaps of red onions grow larger and larger as wholesalers buy and stockpile them in quantity for later shipment outside the area. Similarly, Sarkawa and Kyedyawa sell some of their smoked fish piece by piece in the market, but much of it they bring to buyers waiting nearby who load the bundles onto trucks for resale in other parts of Nigeria.

117

Fulani men drive the cattle they plan to sell to the slaughterhouse and leave them there, for Fulani take no part in the preparation or selling of meat. The cows are quickly killed and butchered by Hausa men, and the meat brought immediately to stalls where hired drummers announce its arrival, since quick sale is vital in this climate. Some butchers skewer small strips of beef for charcoal broiling. Heavily coated with pepper and ground peanuts, the spicy tidbits are sold all day in the marketplace.

Fulani women, quite separate from their men, gather in groups under the shade of neem trees to sell cool soured milk by the dipperful. Refreshing on a hot day, and nourishing as well, this is a drink popular with all the tribespeople. The women sell all they have brought, and then use the money to buy food and clothing and other necessities.

*Beef and soured milk for
sale in Yelwa market*

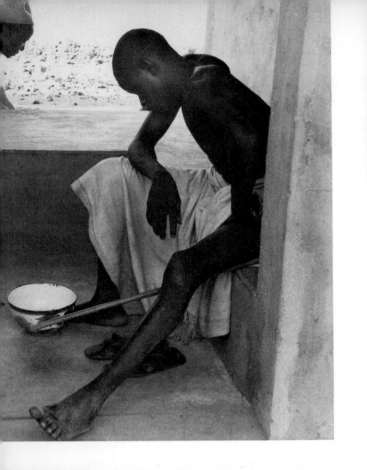

By midmorning the marketplace is full. It is so hot that sweat runs down people's bodies, and each patch of shade is a refuge from the sun. In this small space nearly a dozen tribes are meeting and trading, nearly a dozen languages are being spoken. Some people are almost naked. Some are so covered in robes that only their faces and hands show. Some are dark-skinned, some light. Some speak softly in tones hard to hear over the market din. Others bargain loudly for goods, waving their arms to emphasize a *final* price offered. Babies nurse when hungry, and nap on their mothers' backs. Children watch the activities, play games with beans and stones, or sell their wares from head trays. Young men meet their girls and seek a quiet corner to talk privately. Beggars walk about, shouting for alms from pious Moslems, or sit silently, resting their twisted limbs, their bowls beside them. A town madman laces through the crowds, sweeps his ragged robes across his chest, and mounts a rubbish heap to give a speech. A market woman hands him a tinful of roasted peanuts, for everyone knows that he must live on what others give him. Old women stop to gossip as they go about their business, talking of lazy daughters-in-law, of illnesses in the family, of the price of food.

Now one can clearly see the patterns of specialization and exchange on which the area thrives. Here a Fulani woman chooses what is for her an absolute necessity—a large calabash to hold milk. Farmers of several tribes grow the gourds from which the calabashes are made for sale to Yelwa men, who prepare them according to the tastes of customers. For Fulani, the carvers cut elaborate patterns into the soft shell. The uncut portions are smooth, tan and shiny, while the incised areas are white and dull in texture.

Like Fulani facial tattoos, jewelry, and the embroidery on their clothes, these calabashes reflect a preference for the delicate and linear. Kamberi buy much plainer calabashes, the outside surface often merely polished.

Gourds, easy to raise, inexpensive to buy, are very light in weight, an important consideration when they may be filled with produce and carried many miles. They grow in many different shapes and sizes, and can be made with little difficulty into dippers, spoons, eating dishes, water jugs, beer containers, and grain and flour bowls. Handled with care, they will last for years, and may even be mended with

metal brads when cracked. Everyone uses them; everyone buys them; farmers and carvers earn their living.

Other Yelwa craftsmen make leather goods—hats and purses for Fulani, belts for Kamberi and Gungawa, sandals and knife sheaths for all. At one stall a Kamberi youth fingers a new belt, deciding how much money to offer for it. Nearby a tailor has set up his treadle sewing machine and works on an order, while chatting with Mallam Baba, an old friend. A customer may ask for a garment in the morning and pick it up at the end of the day, paying with the profits from his own goods.

If a person is sick, he will go to a stall where medicines and charms are prepared. Small leather-covered packets of magic substances are sold as protection from illness, accident, bad luck, or the ill wishes of a neighbor. This child wears hers like a necklace, while men and women often have a string of them around the waist.

A great variety of food is sold in the market. Threading their way amongst the crowds, little girls hawk head trays of nuts, bean cakes, peanut pretzels, and small crunchy fried fish. A man pulls taffy around an iron hook held between his toes, and

Foodstuffs for sale in the market

breaks it into small pieces when it has become brittle. From pots bubbling over charcoal fires, town women sell hot spicy stews and bowls of pounded yam, rice, or sorghum. There is even a small shop with a kerosene-powered refrigerator, which sells cold soft drinks—expensive, but popular with local youth. Large stands sell foodstuffs used by all the tribes—salt, flour, bottles full of cooking oil—and utensils as well—sifters, enameled bowls, and kerosene lamps made from evaporated milk cans. Here a Fulani woman pays for her purchase while her baby sleeps securely on her back.

125

Many market stalls are run by merchants who buy
their goods elsewhere for sale in the market. Such
clothing sellers buy finished garments from local
tailors, and handmade cloth from Moslem women
like the weavers shown earlier. Hausa men take
great pride in these finely embroidered hats. A man
will often save his money carefully and pay a part of
the purchase price each week while the hat is being
made.

Still other stalls sell machine-made goods. A steadily increasing amount comes from Nigerian factories, but most are still made in Europe, England, and
the United States. The glass beads and steel swords
that were traded from Europe into African markets
for centuries have been replaced today by nylon
fishnets and floats, plastic dishware and combs,
flashlights, padlocks, metal tools, and bicycles.

126

In the future, more and more factory-made goods will come to Yelwa—radios, electric generators, outboard engines, irrigation pumps, machines of all sorts. Manufacturing in Yelwa itself will become more mechanized, and transportation will be more sophisticated. Information from the rest of the world will be more available in Yelwa via radio, newspapers, and books.

The people of Yelwa and the countryside will change inevitably in the future. But the chances are good that they will continue to flourish, for the principles they have lived by for hundreds of years

In Yelwa one can buy everything from a magic amulet to a bicycle.

are still sound—economic specialization and peaceful exchange, pride in their own culture, and tolerance of great social differences. The Kamberi on his bicycle, the Gungawa with his gasoline-powered pump, the young girls dressed in printed cloth from Japan and performing old tribal dances, the huge trucks carrying home-smoked fish to southern Nigeria—all these show that people here have found a unity in diversity. And they are as adaptable as the waters of the Niger, which, though molded and changed by the dam and the lake, still flow steadily, now as always, across the breadth of West Africa.

Bibliography

BOOKS

Barth, Heinrich. *Travels and Discoveries in North and Central Africa.* London and New York, F. Cass, 1965.

Bohannan, Paul, and Curtin, Philip. *Africa and Africans.* Garden City, The Natural History Press, 1971.

Bohannan, Paul, and Dalton, George, eds. *Markets in Africa.* Evanston, Northwestern University Press, 1962.

Bovill, E. W. *Caravans of the Old Sahara.* London, Oxford University Press, 1933.

——*The Golden Trade of the Moors.* London and New York, Oxford University Press, 1958.

——*The Niger Explored.* London and New York, Oxford University Press, 1968.

Buchanan, K. M., and Pugh, J. C. *Land and People in Nigeria.* London, London University Press, 1955.

Burns, Alan Cuthbert. *History of Nigeria.* London, Allen and Unwin, 1964.

Clapperton, Hugh. *Journal of a Second Expedition into the Interior of Africa.* London, John Murray, 1829.

Coleman, James. *Nigeria: Background to Nationalism.* Berkeley, University of California Press, 1960.

Crowder, Michael. *A Short History of Nigeria.* New York, F. A. Praeger, 1966.

Davidson, Basil. *The African Genius.* Boston and Toronto, Little, Brown, 1969.

——.*The Lost Cities of Africa.* Boston and Toronto, Little, Brown, 1959.

Denham, D., Clapperton, H., and Oudney, W. *Narrative of Travels and Discoveries in Africa.* London, John Murray, 1826.

Fortes, M., and Evans-Pritchard, E. E., eds. *African Political Systems.* London, Oxford University Press, 1940.

Gervis, Pearce. *Of Emirs and Pagans.* London, Cassell, 1963.

Gibbs, James L., ed. *Peoples of Africa.* New York, Holt, Rinehart and Winston, 1965.

Gunn, Harold, and Conant, F. P. *Peoples of the Middle Niger.* London, International African Institute, 1960.

Hatch, John. *Nigeria: The Seeds of Disaster.* Chicago, H. Regnery, 1969.

Hill, Polly. *Studies in Rural Capitalism in West Africa.* Cambridge, England, Cambridge University Press, 1970.

Hogben, S. J., and Kirk-Greene, A. H. M. *The Emirates of Northern Nigeria.* London, Oxford University Press, 1966.

Hopen, C. E. *The Pastoral Fulbe Family in Gwandu.* London, Ibadan, Accra, Oxford University Press, 1958.

Ibn Battuta. *Travels in Asia and Africa, 1325–1354,* translated by H. A. R. Gibb. Cambridge, England, published for the Hakluyt Society at the University Press, 1958.

Lander, Richard and John. *Journal of an Expedition to Explore the Course and Termination of the Niger, etc.* London, John Murray, 1832.

Meek, C. K. *Northern Tribes of Nigeria.* London, Oxford University Press, 1925.

Nadel, S. F. *A Black Byzantium.* London and New York, Oxford University Press, 1942.

Park, Mungo. *Journal of a Mission to the Interior of Africa, in 1805, etc.* London, John Murray, 1815.

———.*Travels in the Interior Districts of Africa, in 1795, 1796 and 1797, etc.* London, Milner, 1799.

Paulme-Schaeffner, Denise, ed. *Women of Tropical Africa.* Berkeley and Los Angeles, University of California Press, 1963.

Smith, Mary. *Baba of Karo.* New York, Philosophical Library, 1955.

Smith, M. G. *The Economy of the Hausa Communities of Zaria.* London, Colonial Office, 1955.

———.*Government in Zazzau, 1800–1950.* London, New York, Toronto, Oxford University Press, 1960.

Stenning, D. J. *Savannah Nomads.* London and Ibadan, Oxford University Press, 1959.

Sterling, Thomas. *Exploration of Africa.* New York, American Heritage, 1963.

Temple, O. and C. L. *Notes on the Tribes, Provinces, Emirates and States of Northern Nigeria.* London and Lagos, The C. M. S. Bookshop, 1922.

Trimingham, H. S. *A History of Islam in West Africa.* London, Oxford University Press, 1962.

———.*Islam in West Africa.* London, Clarendon Press, 1959.

Vlahos, Olivia. *African Beginnings.* New York, Viking, 1967.

PAPERS, PAMPHLETS, AND ARTICLES

Adalemo, I. "The Kainji Dam—A Resettlement." *Nigeria Magazine*, 1968, No. 99, pp. 265–279.

Bazigos, G. P. "Frame Survey at Kainji Lake." Kainji Lake Research Project, Food and Agriculture Organization of the United Nations, Rome, 1970.

Crowder, Michael. "Nigeria's Great Rivers." *Nigeria Magazine,* 1960, No. 64, pp. 28–55.

Ekwensi, Cyprian, "Three Weeks Among the Fulani." *Nigeria Magazine*, 1960, No. 66, pp. 124–133.

Fitzgerald, R. T. D. "The Kakakari Peoples of Sokoto Province." *Man*, 1942 , Vol. XLII, pp. 25–36.

Harris, P. G. "Notes on Yauri (Sokoto Province) Nigeria." *Journal of the Royal Anthropological Institute*, 1930, Vol. LX, pp. 283–334.

Hill, Polly. "Hidden Trade in Hausaland." *Man*, 1969, Vol. 4, pp. 392–409.

————."The Myth of the Amorphous Peasantry—A Northern Nigerian Case Study." *Nigerian Institute of Social and Economic Research Information Bulletin,* 1968, Reprint Series No. 53, pp. 239–260.

Jenness, Jonathan. "Fishermen of the Kainji Basin." Kainji Lake Research Project, Food and Agriculture Organization of the United Nations, Rome, 1970.

————. "Reservoir Resettlement in Africa." Food and Agriculture Organization of the United Nations, Rome, 1969.

Mason, Michael. "Population Density and Slave Raiding—The Case of the Middle Belt of Nigeria." *The Journal of African History,* 1969, Vol. X, No. 4, pp. 551–564.

Meek, C. K. "The Religions of Nigeria." *Africa*, 1943, Vol. XIV, pp. 106–117.

Roder, Wolf, "The Irrigation Farmers of the Kainji Lake Region." Kainji Lake Research Project, Food and Agriculture Organization of the United Nations, Rome, 1970.

St. Croix, F. W. de. *The Fulani of Northern Nigeria.* Lagos, The Government Printer, 1945.

Smith, M. G. "The Social Functions and Meaning of Hausa Praise-singing." *Africa*, 1957, Vol. XXVII, pp. 26–45.

Webster, G. W. "Custom and Beliefs of the Fulani." *Man,* 1931, Vol. XXXI, pp. 238–244.

ABOUT THE AUTHOR

Aylette Jenness gathered the material for this book during the
three years that Nigeria was her home. She lived in several parts
of the country, but it was the town of Yelwa that came to interest
her the most. Her first visit there was during a celebration of the
Fulani tribe, where, she writes, she found herself "more ob-
served than observer. In fact I was poked, stroked, stared at,
patted, and discussed by the Fulani, who showed themselves so
little concerned with me as a fellow human being that I formed
an indelible impression of their unquestioned sense of themselves as superior beings. By the end of the three years, I was
staying in Yelwa in the household of the chief of the fisherman
of the emirate, a Kyedyawa tribesman, warmed by the family's
easy acceptance of me, and delighted by the daily happenings
and rhythms of Yelwa life."

Aylette Jenness is the author of two previous books for young
people, *Gussuk Boy* and *Dwellers of the Tundra*, both about life
in an Eskimo village in Alaska where she stayed for more than a
year. She now lives in Cambridge, Massachusetts.